"Starr Tomczak offers a unique approach to reading and reflecting on Torah, using the lens of her life story to help others connect central scriptural themes and deep spiritual truths with their personal journeys. Her writing is very accessible, yet rich with solid biblical scholarship and supported by contemporary social research. It is an appealing combination that has potential to reach a wide audience."

—MARJORIE J. THOMPSON, author of *Soul Feast: An Invitation to the Christian Spiritual Life*

"Starr Tomczak invites the reader into the Bible with all the wonder, excitement, and lilt of a first-time reader. She interweaves the biblical stories with her own lived experience that she articulates in quite vivid and welcome ways. The outcome of her singular interweaving is a freshness in the biblical material that will be well received by many attentive readers. Tomczak's work is ample testimony to the truth that Scripture is a gift that keeps on giving when it is addressed with trusting imagination."

—WALTER BRUEGGEMANN, William Marcellus McPheeters Professor emeritus of Old Testament, Columbia Theological Seminary

"What an engaging book! It links personal stories of its author with select biblical stories to trace a redemptive journey from hurt to healing, from struggles to insights, from literature to life. Responsible appropriations of Scripture, from Genesis through Deuteronomy, yield amazing interpretations and transformations. Indeed, I found myself binge-reading this book, not for academic reasons but for life enhancement."

—PHYLLIS TRIBLE, professor emerita of sacred literature, Union Theological Seminary

"The book is a unique resource: a truly readable introduction to the Bible by a non-academic for non-academics that draws on up-to-date, high-quality scholarship."

—DAVID CARR, professor of Hebrew Bible, Union Theological Seminary

"Anyone who doubts the relevance of stories in Torah for Christians needs the author's striking account of how her life, in its rough patches and its beauty, has been informed by Scripture. A reader is taken beyond the ideologies and passions that rule our day and invited to enter a world of quiet, uplifting reflection regarding the perplexing issues raised by religion and the language of faith."

—RICHARD CROUTER, professor emeritus of religious studies, Carleton College

"Starr Tomczak uses what she learned from preeminent biblical scholars David Carr and Phyllis Trible at Union Theological Seminary (NYC) to craft often heart-rending reflections on iconic texts in Genesis, Exodus, Leviticus, Numbers, and Deuteronomy. Here she clearly demonstrates that storytelling is a powerful strategy for managing pain, surviving trauma, and handing on a faith not based on dogma promulgated by prelates, but on the stories shared by ordinary people."

—Don C. Benjamin, professor of biblical and Near Eastern studies, Arizona State University

"I was privileged to read drafts of Starr Tomczak's chapters on Exodus and was immediately impressed by the clarity of her writing and the application of her knowledge to her life of faith. I invited her to be a guest leader of an adult education class I was teaching on Exodus, and her presentation of this material made for a powerful session that some participants found personally moving. This book adds immeasurably to our thinking about how to use Exodus devotionally."

—Craig Townsend, Episcopal priest

"The author has found a way to weave a historical-critical understanding of biblical text accessible to the layperson with her own personal story in a way that makes the scholarship come alive with an unusual immediacy and vibrancy. It would be particularly useful for adult study groups or even pre-bar/bat mitzvah students."

—Evan Slavitt, former temple president and Jewish activist

Living Well

Living Well

Inspired by the Story behind the Bible

STARR TOMCZAK

CASCADE Books • Eugene, Oregon

LIVING WELL
Inspired by the Story behind the Bible

Copyright © 2024 Starr Tomczak. All rights reserved. Except for brief quotations in critical publications or reviews, no part of this book may be reproduced in any manner without prior written permission from the publisher. Write: Permissions, Wipf and Stock Publishers, 199 W. 8th Ave., Suite 3, Eugene, OR 97401.

Cascade Books
An Imprint of Wipf and Stock Publishers
199 W. 8th Ave., Suite 3
Eugene, OR 97401

www.wipfandstock.com

PAPERBACK ISBN: 978-1-6667-7185-5
HARDCOVER ISBN: 978-1-6667-7186-2
EBOOK ISBN: 978-1-6667-7187-9

Cataloguing-in-Publication data:

Names: Tomczak, Starr, author.

Title: Living well : inspired by the story behind the Bible / Starr Tomczak.

Description: Eugene, OR: Cascade Books, 2024. | Includes bibliographical references.

Identifiers: ISBN 978-1-6667-7185-5 (paperback). | ISBN 978-1-6667-7186-2 (hardcover). | ISBN 978-1-6667-7187-9 (ebook).

Subjects: LCSH: Bible.—Pentateuch—Criticism, interpretation, etc. | Bible—Hermeneutics.

Classification: BS1225.3 T66 2024 (print). | BS1225.3 (epub)

03/11/24

Unless otherwise indicated, Scripture quotations are taken from the New Revised Standard Version, Updated Edition. Copyright © 2021 National Council of Churches of Christ in the United States of America. Used by permission. All rights reserved worldwide.

Contents

Telling Our Stories   1

PART I. LIVING IN GOD'S IMAGE (FIRST PART OF GENESIS)

1	Created in God's Image	9
2	Happiness in the Garden of Eden	18
3	Darkness outside the Garden	27
4	Justice and Compassion in Noah's Flood	36

PART II. TAKING A JOURNEY (SECOND PART OF GENESIS)

5	Abraham Counting the Stars	47
6	Calling for Isaac's Sacrifice	56
7	Jacob Wrestling with God	64
8	Divine Providence in Joseph's Life	71

PART III. FINDING REDEMPTION (EXODUS)

9	Overcoming Adversity	81
10	Celebrating a Peaceful Victory	90
11	Making It through the Wilderness	99

PART IV. PICTURING THE PROMISED LAND (LEVITICUS, NUMBERS, AND DEUTERONOMY)

12 Drawing Close to God — 109
13 Blessings for the Journey — 117
14 Centering Our Lives — 124
15 Choosing the Best Way — 132

Carrying on the Dream — 141

Endnotes — 143
Acknowledgments — 155
Appendix A: Time Line of Israel's History and the Bible's First Five Books — 157
Appendix B: Questions for Reflection and Discussion — 161
Appendix C: Organizing a Discussion Group — 167
Appendix D: Biblical Passages by Scribes and Priests about the Flood — 169
Bibliography — 173

Telling Our Stories

On a leisurely Saturday morning, I was browsing through the religion section of a bookstore near my home in New York City. Ever since my grandparents had raised me on their farm in Minnesota, they had been my anchor, and now that they had died, I was searching for another anchor.

In the bookstore that morning, I was drawn to the Bible. Although it had served as a lifeline for my grandparents, it had brought me nothing but disappointment. I had hoped Scripture would comfort me during my troubled relationship with my mother and stepfather after they took me from the farm to live with them in Minneapolis, but it never did. By the time I left for college, followed by law school and a long career as a lawyer in New York City, I felt the Bible had little connection to my life.

As I pulled one book after another off the shelf, a study Bible caught my attention. It was the first book I had seen that explained not just what the stories said but also how they were written. The book described who wrote them and when, where, how, and why they wrote them. My view of the Bible completely changed when I discovered that writers told the stories to help people cope with problems they faced in their communities. For the first time, I realized that the stories were written for people like me to help them through difficulties like mine. Looking at the Bible this way makes it easier for all of us to relate the stories to our experiences. Instead of getting bogged down by archaic language, ancient cultural norms, or an overly literal approach, we can see how the fundamental points raised by the stories apply to our lives today.

Telling Our Stories

I find this insight so powerful that I am writing this book to provide a springboard for you to relate the Bible to your own experiences. To help you connect the Bible to your life, I focus on a key point of each biblical narrative and show why the point mattered to the people writing the story. To bring the story into our world today, I relate it to my life, and I put it in a broader context by including Jewish, Christian, and secular views and social science research. The discussion blends religious and historical observations with personal narrative, psychological insights, and sociological perspectives.

Take the exodus, for example. As told in the Bible, the exodus is a story about God rescuing the Israelites from bondage under an Egyptian pharaoh. They included six hundred thousand men on foot, which together with women, children, and the elderly would be more than two million people. When the Egyptian army cornered the Israelites against the sea, God parted the waters of the sea so that the Israelites could escape by walking on dry land. The story is about freedom and justice for the Israelite slaves, it is key to Jewish identity, and it is part of the Christian story of salvation. But the event is so huge and spectacular that I wondered whether it really happened, and even if it did, I wondered how it mattered in my much more ordinary life.

Looking at the origins of the exodus story answers these concerns. From a historical perspective, many scholars conclude that the exodus story is based on real events. Its significance to the Israelites since early times, its historical context, and details like the Egyptian name of Moses all suggest the story actually happened. But no written records or archaeological finds back up the large exodus of the Israelites recounted in the Bible. Given the lack of evidence for the size of the exodus in the biblical account, the actual exodus probably involved a smaller number of people who had been captured by Egyptians and were working as slaves in fields and military installations.

After the exodus, the Israelites kept telling the story because it resonated with their community. Upon leaving Egypt, the escaped slaves settled in villages in what is now Israel and praised God for saving them. Their story inspired other villagers who likewise had been dominated by Egyptian or other powerful groups. Eventually all the villagers adopted the story as their own, giving them confidence to resist attacks and overcome setbacks. To stress the significance of the exodus to future generations, the Israelites expanded the story by emphasizing the size of the event. Throughout many centuries, the story was originally passed along by word of mouth, later written down, enlarged, and revised, and finally included in the Bible.

Just as the Israelite community did, we can make the story of divine deliverance our own. Redemption can mean deliverance from sin, as Christians tend to emphasize, or deliverance from harm, as the exodus story emphasizes. When we struggle with adversity, the story offers hope that we can break free. It provides inspiration to overcome troubled pasts, broken relationships, economic hardships, and other barriers to becoming the person we are meant to be.

For me, the exodus story relates to God saving me through my grandparents' love from the damaging effects of parental abuse. My grandparents provided a refuge from my parents and encouraged a better direction for my life. But for my grandparents' love, my parents' mistreatment would have had far worse consequences.

My quest to relate the biblical stories to my life was driven by nostalgia for my grandparents' farm. Since I was a young child, the farm was a safe haven where I felt God's love and learned to cherish Scripture. While I lived there with my grandparents, my grandfather's parents, and my uncle and aunt, my relatives kept their Bibles on top of their dressers in the bedrooms and took the Bibles down to read in quiet times of grief, anxiety, or devotion. On a nearby farm, my grandmother's father kept his Bible on the side table next to his armchair in the living room. There he alternated between Scripture passages and *Newsweek* magazine, watched the news on television, and talked with visitors about political and religious matters of the day. With enormous pride, my grandmother told me that he had read the entire Bible several times, and "even the ministers in town marvel at how well he knows it."

If I had stayed on the farm while growing up, the Bible might have become my bedrock in the same way it had been for my grandparents. But my life changed dramatically when my mother and stepfather took me to live with them in Minneapolis after I reached school age. At first, they seemed aloof in a house that lacked any warmth, and then they became increasingly abusive. Looking for consolation, I spotted a Bible next to the knickknacks in the living room and read all fifty chapters of its first book, Genesis. Instead of finding comfort, I felt overwhelmed by the massive effort I had made and how little it had helped me. So I turned to schoolwork to distract me from the chaos at my house, and after high school, I left home for

Carleton College fifty miles away. Eventually I attended law school at New York University and became a lawyer in New York City.

After my grandparents died many years later, I tried to rekindle the reverence I once had for Scripture. First, I attended a few Bible study classes, but just like my childhood attempts at reading the Bible, the people, places, and events in the stories seemed so removed from my experience that I could not yet see their relevance to me. Trying a different approach, I organized a discussion group to talk about the spiritual side of life with my Christian, Jewish, and secular friends. I was looking for background reading for the group when I discovered the study Bible that described how the Bible was written.

Finding this new way to read the Bible was so enthralling that I reduced my law practice and enrolled in a master of divinity program at Union Theological Seminary in New York City. For more than a century, Union has been at the forefront of historical studies of the Bible's origins. Back in 1891, Charles Briggs, a Union professor and Presbyterian pastor, gave a controversial lecture on the topic. Intrigued by European scholarship about the Bible's origins, Briggs disagreed with the traditional Jewish and Christian view that Moses had written the Bible's first five books. Historical studies suggested instead that these books had been written by several authors, resulting in repetitions and inconsistencies, and reflecting cultural views at odds with scientific and historical facts. Even though Briggs considered the Bible infallible on matters of faith and practice, that was not enough to satisfy the Presbyterian Church. In 1893, the church found him guilty of heresy for teaching that Scripture may have errors.[1]

By the time I attended Union, the Presbyterian Church (USA), along with many other Protestant, Catholic, and Jewish groups, had accepted historical studies of how the Bible was written.[2] These studies have focused on the biblical text in its historical, social, cultural, linguistic, and religious context. Considering these studies, religious groups have realized that biblical writers reflected their time and place, and consequently, learning about their context gives us a better understanding of the Bible. Yet accepting the Bible's origins from a historical perspective does not mean rejecting Scripture as "the word of God." Like me, many people of faith believe the text is divinely inspired even though the writers were influenced by their historical setting.

In this book, we focus on the Bible's first five books traditionally assumed to be written by Moses—Genesis, Exodus, Leviticus, Numbers, and

Deuteronomy. These books are known to Jews as the Torah (Hebrew for "teachings") and to Christians as the Pentateuch (Greek for "five books"). They are a key part of the Hebrew Bible, which is called the Old Testament by Christians and the Tanakh by Jews. Since Jesus lived in a Jewish community, the Torah shaped his religious upbringing as well as the perspective of people writing the New Testament.

Even though this book discusses the biblical stories in the order they appear in the Bible, we know these stories were composed at different times and places before they were arranged in this sequence. The Israelite tribes initially told stories about their escape from Egypt and the feats of their ancestors. After David and Solomon formed a monarchy, the royal court began adapting creation and flood stories of the ancient Near East to Israelite views. When the Assyrians later threatened the Israelites, the surviving Israelites expressed their allegiance to God alone in what Jews call the Shema and Christians call the Great Commandment. In a devastating blow, the Babylonians subsequently destroyed Jerusalem and marched the Israelites to live in exile in Babylon. Their years of exile became one of the most fruitful periods of the Bible's development, as the exilic writers comforted the Israelites by conveying God's assurance of a promising future.

During my time at Union, my professor David Carr, a leading specialist on how the Bible was written, explained why he thought the biblical stories remain so compelling. In contrast to the victorious kings and capital cities along with their gods in other ancient Near Eastern texts, the Israelites were underdogs surrounded at first by the great empires of Egypt, Assyria, and Babylonia and later by the Persians, Greeks, and Romans. Israel was besieged, destroyed, and rebuilt, and its people lived through slavery, exile, and oppression. Their stories helped them overcome traumatic experiences in a catastrophic world. When we read their stories today, many of us still find hope to survive and thrive no matter our difficulties.[3]

Like any historical study, the description of the Bible's development in this book is not intended to be definitive but rather suggestive of a likely way it occurred. To help you keep in mind the historical events that influenced the writing of the Bible, appendix A includes a time line connecting Israel's history with the origins of the Bible's first five books. When I recount stories from my personal experiences, I relate them to the best of my knowledge while changing names and identifying details of other people.

Each chapter of this book begins with a reference to biblical passages discussed in the chapter. For translation of the original text, unless otherwise noted, I use the New Revised Standard Version, Updated Edition (NRSVue) reflecting the Christian tradition. The New Jewish Publication Society (NJPS) translation of the Tanakh is well regarded in the Jewish tradition. If you do not have a Bible, many translations are available on free websites and apps.

This book is intended for people looking for inspiration in the biblical stories for their personal lives. If you assume God dictated the Bible word by word, I hope you will consider a broader view of divine inspiration. If you are spiritually curious or downright skeptical, studying the origins of the biblical stories is a good introduction to the text because historical studies do not presume faith in God. Whether you attribute the stories to the human spirit or divine inspiration, you can consider their relevance to your life. For further insights relating the text to your life, appendices B and C have questions for reflection and discussion as well as pointers for discussion groups.

Learning how the Bible was written has helped me make sense of my life and the world around us. Given the pandemic and economic difficulties of the past few years, many people are reassessing what is most important to them. By exploring the Bible in a new way, I hope you will discover how it can guide you to a more fulfilling life.

PART I

Living in God's Image

(First Part of Genesis)

1

Created in God's Image

How does the notion of creation in God's image affect the way you see yourself and others?

GENESIS 1:1—2:3 (CREATION)

My MOTHER BURST INTO the farmhouse just as my great-grandparents, grandparents, uncle, and I had finished eating dinner. Great-Grandpa was sitting in his rocking chair by the kitchen table, while Grandpa and Uncle Bill were still at the table, all the men wearing the overalls they had pulled on at five o'clock in the morning to milk the cows and work in the fields. The women in their housedresses were clearing the table and washing the dishes. I was playing on the floor by the rocking chair with a toy tractor Grandpa had given me when he bought a full-size John Deere for the farm.

Grandma looked worried as Mom cornered her on the other side of the room. Mom was wearing a halter top and short shorts, her red lipstick offset by heavy mascara, and her dark brown hair swept behind her ears and up into two large curls above her forehead. Great-Grandpa grumbled about her shorts, said "Umph," and left the room. Great-Grandma concentrated on the dishes. The others huddled around Mom, trying to keep things calm.

I kept to the sidelines with my toy tractor. Still, I could hear the conversation was about me. Mom was angry because I had missed almost all of kindergarten even though I was already six years old. She blamed the "hick town" by the farm for being so backward it did not have one. Since

I had never heard of kindergarten, I did not think it mattered. Even so, I wondered why no one had thought about it before then.

A week later, my grandparents packed my belongings, drove me sixty-six miles northeast to Minneapolis, and left me in a house I had never seen before where Mom lived with her new husband. The next day I went to my first day of kindergarten. It was so late in the school year that the class was coloring Easter eggs. Although I enjoyed playing with new toys and other kids, I could not wait until Grandpa and Grandma picked me up to take me back to the farm for Easter vacation.

Until this point, I had lived mostly in the country with my great-grandparents, grandparents, and Uncle Bill, soon to marry my aunt. Even though we were crowded together in an old farmhouse without indoor plumbing, I had an idyllic life. I rode on hay wagons hitched to horses, helped the women cut beans, shell peas, and pick raspberries, and played with the dogs and cats in the barn while the men milked the cows. Every now and then, Grandpa and Grandma would take me to the swings and slide at the park in town, and Sunday mornings the whole family would go to the Lutheran church near the park. At the end of each day, Grandma would tell me a story, say a prayer, and kiss me good night.

Even if the nearby town did not have kindergarten, its schooling was typical of rural areas. My great-grandparents had gone to country school through third grade, my grandparents had gone to school in town through eighth grade, and my mother and uncle had graduated from high school. Granted, no one ever bought any books. But each person kept the Bible and prayer book given at confirmation in the Lutheran church.

Before Mom's sudden obsession with kindergarten, I could not recall seeing her more than a couple times, and I had no memories of her ever hugging me, talking to me, or showing interest in anything I did. So her rage about school surprised me. Many years later as an adult, I pieced together the cause of her obsession. While she had been married to my father, she had had one reason after another for not taking care of me—I was colicky, she was anemic, she disapproved of the childcare near her work. After she married my stepfather, my grandparents feared that she would take me away from them. But that did not happen until my stepfather, badly in debt, negotiated an up-front cash payment from my father in exchange for providing my future support. To keep up my stepfather's end of the bargain, my mother moved me in with her to go to kindergarten, and my father, whom I did not remember anyway, vanished from my childhood. From then on,

Created in God's Image

I stayed in the city during the school week and spent weekends, Easter and Christmas vacations, and summers on the farm throughout grade school and often during high school.

Every time Grandpa and Grandma took me back to the city, I felt as though I was going to stay with strangers in a place where I did not belong. Since my mother and stepfather did not want their propriety questioned by the neighbors, I could not say that Mom had been divorced, my stepfather was not my real dad, and I had not been living with either of them until then. As long as I was in grade school, Mom tried to perform her maternal role by serving family dinners every night, watching the Miss America pageant with me, and telling me to balance a book on my head for perfect posture. While Mom went through the motions of what she thought a mother should be, she seemed oblivious to my actual interests and needs. My stepfather would drive me to church and movies with my friends but then forget to pick us up until everyone else had left. Long after the pastor locked the church door and went home or the manager locked the movie theater on his way out the door, my friends and I would be waiting for my stepfather to return. If anyone asked, I would explain that my dad was always late.

My stepfather's back rubs were another problem. Shortly after I moved in, he started offering to give me a back rub. I found the offer appealing, mostly because of the absence of any other affection in the house. But every time he gave me a back rub, his hands would start wandering toward my chest. When I tried to block him by clamping my arms tight against the sides of my body, his hands would keep inching forward underneath my arms along my sides. As soon as that happened, I would jump up and run out of the room. After some time went by, he would make another offer, and I would accept in the hope it would be different this time. It never was.

Far from the warmth of the farm, in Minneapolis I was living in a cold and empty house with no one who cared about me. Searching for comfort, I spotted a Bible on a shelf in the living room. Since the book meant a lot to Grandma, I wondered if I could find in the text what was missing from my life. But no matter how many times I pulled it off the shelf and tried to read it, I could not find what I needed.

When reading the creation story at the beginning of the Bible, I had not realized that the story was intended to inspire people who, like me, were displaced and discouraged. Just as I had been taken from the farmhouse to a strange city, the Israelites had been forced to march from their homes in

Jerusalem to exile in Babylon. The glorious city where David and Solomon once reigned had been demolished by the Babylonians. To comfort exiles living in anguish, the Israelite priests wrote a narrative that described how men and women were created in God's image to rule the earth like kings.[4]

There, on the Bible's first few pages, is the startling assertion that everyone is made in God's image. The essential meaning of this concept is the dignity and significance of each person. Ever since the concept was written in Scripture, it has been a boon to people facing trying circumstances. The text affirms our inherent worth no matter how poorly we are treated. Even if we feel relatively powerless, we share with the rest of humanity a likeness to God.

THE BIBLE'S STORY

The creation story in the first chapter of Genesis is notable for its sheer beauty and elegance. God is portrayed as a powerful, majestic king who simply utters commands and, by divine word, creates the world. At first, while a wind swept over dark, watery chaos, God said, "Let there be light," and there was light.[5] On the second day, the Lord made a dome called sky, which created space for the creation by separating an upper ocean above the dome from a lower ocean underneath the earth. The next day the seas were separated from the earth, which completed the basic structure of sky, earth, and seas. On the fourth day, God set the sun, moon, and stars in the dome of the sky to regulate day and night, seasons, and years. By the fifth and sixth days, birds flew across the sky; fish and sea creatures swarmed the waters; and cattle, wild animals, and creeping things roamed the earth.

Now that God had set the stage, the final act on the sixth day was the creation of human beings. God said to a divine council: "Let us make humanity as our image, similar to our likeness *so that* they may rule the fish of the sea, the birds of the heavens, the cattle and all the earth, and all the creatures creeping on the earth."[6] After that, "God created humans in his image, / in the image of God he created them; / male and female he created them," and then God blessed them and said, "Be fruitful and multiply and fill the earth and subdue it and have dominion over the fish of the sea and over the birds of the air and over every living thing that moves upon the earth."[7] God called all this work very good and rested on the seventh day.

Some modern readers have been astounded that such an ancient text has so much respect for every man and woman that each one is seen as

God's image. Through the ages, people have debated whether this means we look like God, represent God on earth, or have moral, spiritual, or other qualities like God. To the ancient Israelites, the text suggested a physical representation of God akin to a king representing God. In ancient times, the king was said to be the "image" of a god and thus acted with divine authority. The biblical creation story takes a more democratic approach. Instead of a king, every person is made in God's image to exercise godlike rule over the earth and its creatures.[8]

Giving people "dominion" over the earth is disturbing to some people these days because they believe it encourages environmental destruction. But the term as used in the story refers to authority to act on God's behalf. In the Bible, people do not own nature but rather act as its steward, accountable to God as the true owner.[9] Typically royalty would claim "dominion" to extend God's care. For example, Psalm 72:8–12 upholds a king's dominion because "he delivers the needy when they call, the poor and those who have no helper." In the creation story, not a king, but ordinary men and women are responsible for taking care of the earth.

The story must have astonished the Israelites. Despite their defeat in Jerusalem and exile in Babylon, they were still special, and they had an important job to do. God affirmed their dignity, gave them a purpose, and endowed them with the power and creativity needed for their responsibilities. While the Israelites should not yield to despair, neither should they gloat over their superiority. Even their captors had the mark of divinity and should be held in the same regard. This exalted status of every individual appears to be unique in the ancient world and remains a powerful incentive for human rights to this day.

WRITING THE STORY

I find it remarkable that such an uplifting story about creation in God's image was written down during the defeat and anguish of the Babylonian exile. Before we begin to reconstruct how this story was written, I want to reiterate that even when we study the story from a historical perspective, we can still acknowledge a religious dimension. As a person of faith, I believe that God created men and women in God's image and that the writers of the biblical text were divinely inspired. Perhaps the Babylonian exile was the perfect time to write this creation story because the exiles badly needed encouragement, or perhaps the priests at that time were best suited to write the story in a way that would resonate with future generations. Although we cannot know how the biblical writers were divinely inspired, we can study the historical and cultural developments that influenced their writings.

To understand the creation account from a historical perspective, we look to the great cultures of Egypt along the Nile River and of Mesopotamia (now mostly Iraq) between the Tigris and Euphrates Rivers. By 3000 BCE, these regions had developed cities and introduced writing.[10] While the Egyptian rulers maintained some continuity, Mesopotamia was initially dominated by the Sumerians, later the Assyrians, and then the Babylonians. In the Bible, the area between these Egyptian and Mesopotamian superpowers was called Canaan. This area eventually became the homeland of ancient Israel and its neighbors.

By around 1000 BCE, Israel had formed a monarchy ruled from Jerusalem by David and then Solomon. Under their reigns, scribes joined the royal court, writing was introduced, and prominent Israelites learned about Egyptian and Mesopotamian texts. Emulating other Near Eastern cultures, Solomon built a magnificent temple attended by influential priests. After Solomon died, the area divided into a Northern Kingdom and a Southern Kingdom. Later, the Assyrians demolished the Northern Kingdom and threatened Jerusalem's rule over the Southern Kingdom. Then the Babylonians rose to power. They conquered Jerusalem and destroyed its temple around 586 BCE, and marched its royal family, scribes, priests, and other leaders to live in exile in Babylon. The once-glorious kingdom of David and Solomon lay in ruins.

While the Israelite priests were in Babylon, they tried to make sense of Jerusalem's defeat and give hope to exiles living in despair. To the extent that the priests considered the texts of Mesopotamia and Egypt, they would have found little consolation. The cultures of these superpowers glorified their kings and capital cities and the gods that protected them. The priests would need a radically different approach to give hope to the exiles.

When writing the creation story, the Israelite priests seemed familiar with the Enuma Elish, which was compiled around 1100 BCE to celebrate Babylon, its rulers, and its divine patron Marduk.[11] In this epic, a freshwater god merged with a saltwater goddess, resulting in watery chaos out of which a divine assembly of younger gods was born. Rising from this assembly, Marduk and his father killed both the freshwater god and saltwater goddess. Then Marduk took over the assembly, and his command determined all things. He used half of the saltwater goddess's body to make the heavens and the other half to make the earth. Once a domed sky sealed out watery chaos, he assigned the moon and stars to mark the night, months, and seasons. Afterward, Marduk and his father freed the assembly by creating people called "savages" to do its work.

Like the Enuma Elish, the biblical story begins with watery chaos, emphasizes the divine word, describes a domed sky over the earth, regulates seasons with the moon and stars, and completes creation with human beings. But in contrast to the Babylonian epic, the biblical story does not present a conflict between divine powers. It simply portrays one God present from the beginning of time. The biblical story also has a very different ending. It does not refer to people as "savages" who would be the deity's slaves. To the contrary, men and women are created in God's image to care for the world in God's stead.

Another ancient Near Eastern tradition helps to explain the Israelite priests' view of people made in a divine image. In both Babylonian and Egyptian culture, a king was made in the image of a god, and this image embodied in the king was a sign of his authority to rule others. A Mesopotamian letter to the king said: "The father of the king, my lord, was the image of [the god] Bel, and the king, my lord, is likewise the image of Bel." Similarly, in an Egyptian text, the god Amon proclaimed to the king: "You are my beloved son, who came forth out of my love, my image that I set on earth. I let you rule the land in peace."[12]

Although the Israelite priests used the same concept of God's image, they radically changed its application. Instead of glorifying royalty, the priests glorified every man and woman. No other document from that period known to historians claimed that all men and women, not just royalty, were made in God's image.

The Israelite priests had no interest in buttressing the ruling authority, which, after all, had destroyed Jerusalem and forced its people into exile. Under these circumstances, the priests wanted to give hope to exiles living in anguish. However poorly they were treated and however powerless they felt, no one should feel discouraged, because everyone reflects divinity. According to a rabbinic saying, whenever a man or woman walks down the street, he or she is preceded by an invisible choir of angels crying, "Make way, make way! Make way for the image of God."[13]

PART I | LIVING IN GOD'S IMAGE

LIVING BY THE STORY

The Israelite priests surely knew that all people fall short of their godlike potential. Among other atrocities, the Babylonians had killed the sons of Jerusalem's king right before the king's eyes and then gouged out his own eyes, shackled him, and brought him to Babylon.[14] Neither the cruelty of the Babylonians nor the suffering of this king and his children reflected God's vision for creation. In later years, both Judaism and Christianity developed doctrines to help people live in God's image. For guidance, Jews look to the Torah, the teachings in the Bible's first five books, and Christians look to Jesus as the truest image of God.

But even if we do not live up to these ideals, the Israelite priests seemed to grasp that our present situation does not define who we really are. No matter how poorly we are treated or treat others, we are meant for something better. When faced with trying circumstances, we should not forget our inherent worth. Instead of feeling displaced and lost, we can use our creativity and freedom to make our lives better. Instead of feeling mistreated and disparaged, we can remember our self-worth. When other people aggravate us, we can remind ourselves that they too were made to reflect divinity.

When I discussed creation in God's image with my friends, the inspiration they found in the concept illustrates its breadth. Dan, a lawyer known for his brilliant defense of clients, was thrilled to liken himself to God. Although he was proud of his Jewish heritage, he bristled at its rules and rituals. Like a defense attorney before a jury, he paced the room to persuade me, "If we're created to be like God, we have power and imagination to make our lives what we want them to be." As he pictured our true character, we are bold, inventive, and free.

My friend Emily felt kinship with exiled Israelites recovering from a blow to their self-esteem. Ever since she had polio in childhood, she has walked with one shoulder higher than the other. Although she grew up in a Protestant home, no one ever taught her that she was made in God's image. Over the years, she had difficulty appreciating the beauty of her body, the joy of physical movement, and pleasure in life itself. As she explained, "I never trusted my body." She had major surgery on her back at the age of six, additional surgeries as an adult, and more limitations as she grew older. She felt buffeted by doctors who warned against strenuous activity causing further damage yet urged her to watch her weight and exercise. In response, she shunned the physical aspects of her life and focused on its spiritual, mental, and social side. But the Bible gave her another perspective. As she considered the creation story, she realized that divinity comes in many forms, and she could find in her appearance a reflection of God's image. Regardless of the practical limitations of her body, she did not need to see herself as disfigured for she was just as beautiful as any other person made in God's image. In a slightly wavering voice, she proclaimed, "We are *all* made in God's image."

My friend Emma, a lapsed Catholic who questioned whether God existed, was swayed by the moral significance of treating everyone as the image of God. At first, her anger toward the church's doctrines on abortion, divorce, and homosexuality and cover-up of pedophile priests spurred a negative response to creation in God's image. "Why would I believe that?" she snapped. After pausing to consider the concept, she changed her question to ask instead, "What would it actually mean to be created in God's image?" She finally settled on its moral implications: "If everyone were made in God's image, everybody should be treated with dignity."

After reaching this conclusion, Emma admitted that she still appreciated one aspect of her Catholic upbringing—its emphasis on peace and social justice. She was proud that the Catholic Church advocated for immigrants, Pope John Paul II had opposed the Iraq war before it had even started, and Pope Francis has criticized the disparity between the rich and the poor. Even though she considered herself a secular humanist, her values found common ground with religious concepts that recognized divinity in each of us.

I now wish that I had known in grade school how much strength I could have found as a child created in God's image. Although displaced and alone, I was meant to be special with a promising future. I was someone who mattered. Sometimes we cannot help but feel battered down. Yet even in those moments, like the Babylonian exiles, we can lift ourselves back up if we remember the person we are meant to be. When we walk down the street, the angels are saying, "Make way, make way! Make way for the image of God."

2

Happiness in the Garden of Eden

How much happiness have you found in relationships that reinforce a spiritual dimension of life?

GENESIS 2:4–25 (GARDEN OF EDEN)

MY COUSIN'S HUSBAND, MATT, then farming the land with Uncle Bill, picked me up from the airport on one of my many trips back to Minnesota from New York. As Matt and I chatted on the way to the farm, we decided to take a quiz on happiness in a magazine I had brought along for my flight.

I read the questions while Matt drove. Each question included some variation of whether our lives were happy. Possible responses ranged from describing our lives as almost perfect to not at all what we wanted. For question after question, Matt said his life was almost perfect.

I was shocked by Matt's responses. He had been living with kidney failure for more than a decade. Matt spent at least ten hours a day hooked up to a dialysis machine. His illness had interfered with his lifestyle, work, and income. How could he describe his life as "almost perfect"?

As I began to ponder this question, I already knew the answer. Matt loved to farm, he had a wonderful wife and two children, and he was involved in his church and community. Any time I saw him at church, he was making a video of the service so that people could watch it at the local hospital and senior facility. He was a founding member of a club that organized volunteers to work on service projects in town, and year after year, he maintained perfect attendance at club meetings. He was so engaged in doing what he wanted to do that he never complained about his health.

Matt followed in the footsteps of one generation after another on my grandparents' farm. Farming was the most satisfying life anyone could imagine, and every marriage lasted through sickness and health. Well into her eighties, Grandma still referred to Grandpa as "such a good-looking man." Even though farm work never ended and finances were tight, there was always enough time and money to help out a neighbor or visit a relative going through hard times. As the highlight of the week, the entire family from the youngest to the oldest generation would attend worship services in town on Sunday mornings.

Matt's doctors at the renowned Mayo Clinic would not have been surprised that he scored high on happiness despite his health problems. According to the clinic's staff, happiness depends more on attitude than circumstances. The staff finds that people are happier when they feel a sense of purpose, devote time to family and friends, and cultivate gratitude, optimism, and living in the moment. The staff says spirituality can help us clarify our life's purpose by focusing on our connections with others, our search for meaning, and our personal values. If we feel part of a greater whole, we can find inner peace by sharing the burdens of tough times and joys of life's blessings.[15]

For Matt and my other relatives on the farm, their life purpose centered on their faith. It strengthened their connections to family and friends, gave meaning to the work they did on the farm and in their church and community, and kept unfolding new possibilities for living to the utmost. Right before Matt died of kidney-related complications, he told his wife that he saw Jesus calling him to heaven.

The story of the garden of Eden in Genesis 2 describes in a short vignette what I recall about life at its best on the farm. Eden was an idyllic place where Adam and Eve had a joyful romance, satisfying work taking care of the garden, and intimacy with a loving God. The story suggests a sacred, spiritual, or special dimension of life that leads to our fulfillment. Although we cannot return to the garden in its idyllic location, some seek glimmers of its bliss in this life, and some envision its bliss in an afterlife.

PART I | LIVING IN GOD'S IMAGE

THE BIBLE'S STORY

The harmonious life of Adam and Eve with each other, nature, and the Lord provides a divine vision of how we are meant to live. If we jump ahead too quickly to the couple's downfall, we may overlook these ties. But if we consider the couple before then, we can appreciate their enjoyment of life when free from destructive tendencies.

An early version of the story about the garden of Eden may have been written by Israelite scribes in the royal court as far back as the time of Solomon.[16] As told in Genesis 2, their story differs considerably from the creation account in Genesis 1 written by the priests after the monarchy's destruction. The scribes' references to God also differ. While the priests used a general word for God (in Hebrew *elohim*), the scribes identified God by his name YHWH, which is pronounced "Yahweh." Since Jewish tradition considered God's name too sacred to pronounce, biblical translations typically substitute the word Lord, with the initial large capital letter followed by small capital letters.

In contrast to the priests' description of a majestic God creating the cosmos by decree, in the scribes' account, God took a hands-on approach to set up a fulfilling way of life. The story begins by saying plants were not yet in the fields for Yahweh had not caused any rain, and no one was there to till the ground. Then Yahweh formed the first human (in Hebrew *adam*) from the earth (in Hebrew *adamah*) and breathed into the human's nostrils the breath of life. In a single gesture, the divine breath demonstrated the creator's life-giving force, tenderness toward humans, and close connection to the earth and its people. After that, Yahweh planted a magnificent garden and put the human in the garden to till and care for it.

Then Yahweh said it was not good that the human should be alone and decided to make a "helper as his partner."[17] At first, Yahweh made cattle and every other animal and bird and brought them to the human. But none of them were suitable as a partner. Then the creator caused a deep sleep to fall upon the human, took his rib, and made it into another being. Elated, the human exclaimed that his new companion was "bone of my bones and flesh of my flesh" and called her "woman" (in Hebrew *ishah*) for she was taken out of "man" (in Hebrew *ish*). Therefore, the story concludes that a man leaves his parents and "clings to his wife, and they become one flesh."[18]

Sadly, the intimacy of the story was obscured by the Judeo-Christian view that women were subordinate because they were made from Adam's rib to be his helper. Back in 1897, this rationale seemed dubious to Hanna Solomon. As part of a newly formed organization that became the National Council of Jewish Women, she supported major responsibilities for women in public life as well as inside the home. She was certain that women were up to the task. With a touch of humor, she explained that God did not create a woman out of dust. Instead, she said, "The Lord waited until he could build her out of a strong, healthy, germproof bone."[19]

In a groundbreaking work, Phyllis Trible, a biblical scholar at my alma mater Union Theological Seminary in New York City, reexamines the patriarchal view of women as second class, made from Adam's rib to be his helper.[20] As she points out, this view overlooks Adam's obvious joy in finding a true partner. She further notes that gender was not differentiated until both a woman (*ishah*) and a man (*ish*) were formed. To the extent humankind was considered the culmination of creation in Genesis 1, a woman created after man would be the culmination of creation in Genesis 2.

To buttress women's equality, Trible demonstrates that the Hebrew word translated as "helper" does not imply subordination. In fact, when Hebrew Scripture uses the word for help, fifteen of the twenty-one times refer to God's help, and the remaining times aside from this narrative refer to the inadequacy of human help.[21] Nor does modern usage imply that a "helper" is always subordinate. When a parent helps a child, or a teacher helps a student, or a lawyer helps a client, the parent, teacher, and lawyer are not considered subordinate.

Read without patriarchal assumptions, Adam and Eve's story is a blissful romance. As long as Adam and Eve were not drawn to evil, their life was joyful, tender, and spontaneous. Happiness had found its home in the garden.

WRITING THE STORY

After the Israelites formed a monarchy around 1000 BCE, scribes joined the royal court and priests served in the temple. The priests' involvement in religious rituals seemed to give them a more elevated view of human aspirations than the down-to-earth perspective of the scribes who were leaders and scholars in the court. Although scribes were sometimes priests or affiliated with priests, the term *priests* as used in this book refers to priests and their associates, while *scribes* refers to people who were not associated with priests.[22]

Bringing prestige to the court, the scribes were skilled in reading and writing texts and familiar with ancient Near Eastern literature. In the early days of the monarchy, they showed little interest in stories like the exodus that had been passed along by word of mouth from one generation to the next in Israelite tribes. Instead, the scribes concentrated on the literature of Egypt and Mesopotamia. These cultures valued stories about creation and a flood, epics about legendary characters, and pithy sayings to instill wisdom. At the beginning of the Israelite monarchy, the scribes began to adapt Egyptian and Mesopotamian texts to Israelite views, and after the monarchy divided and ended, they continued to develop Israelite works.

The Gilgamesh epic of Mesopotamia was an important text that may have influenced the scribes' portrayal of Adam and Eve.[23] The epic as passed down to us was composed between 2000 and 1800 BCE. In the epic, Gilgamesh, the king of a Sumerian city, was such a tyrant that the residents pleaded for help from the divine assembly. In response, the divine assembly made from clay a male called Enkidu to be Gilgamesh's companion on daring adventures away from the residents. But Enkidu lived like a savage, running with wild animals. To rectify the situation, the divine assembly sent a wise woman to teach him how to be human. The wise woman treated the savage like a man, made love with him, and consequently filled his mind with new wisdom. Then she clothed him and urged him to eat bread and drink beer. After he grew cheerful and groomed himself, the story concludes that he was finally human. Far from taking a subordinate role, the wise woman had been Enkidu's mentor.

Beyond the Gilgamesh epic, James L. Kugel, a professor emeritus of Hebrew literature at Harvard University, provides an intriguing account of the scribes' portrayal of Adam and Eve's relationship with the divine.[24] Kugel suggests that the Lord's intimacy with Adam and Eve reflects extremely ancient notions of close-knit interactions among gods and people. He contrasts the Lord's portrayal in this story with the way God is described in other parts of Hebrew Scripture and the way we conceptualize God in the modern world.

As Kugel explains, many people today consider God all-powerful, all-knowing, and present everywhere. Although Hebrew Scripture seemed to anticipate this view, it never explicitly stated it and often portrayed God with more human characteristics. In the typical Hebrew text, God may be powerful, but not all-knowing or present everywhere. The Lord usually resided in a separate realm, sometimes breaking out to interact with people, sometimes inhabiting a temple or shrine attended by priests, and sometimes staying in a heavenly sphere. As illustrated by the creation story in Genesis 1, for example, God seemed to be a voice without a body, issuing commands that were mysteriously carried out. After giving orders for each step of creation, God inspected the results and was pleased, as if observing from the sidelines.

Compared with God's portrayal in other parts of Hebrew Scripture, the garden of Eden story suggests to Kugel a much more ancient view of God from a far earlier period. Kugel goes back to a time when people had little understanding of what causes events to happen in the world and a limited concept of themselves as individuals capable of determining a course of action. They saw themselves surrounded on all sides, endlessly acted upon by whatever was beyond their control and comprehension. To the extent they contemplated themselves and their surroundings, they must have had an overwhelming sense of their own smallness in a much larger, very active world.

In Kugel's view, the story of Adam and Eve is reminiscent of such a time. The Lord seemed to surround them in a world beyond their control. Forces outside of themselves kept determining what would occur next. In this mysterious setting, God was an overwhelming presence. Yahweh did not appear to reside in a separate realm as suggested by other stories in Hebrew Scripture. He seemed to be walking around *inside* the garden, not coming and going from a heavenly abode, but always there. God was involved in everything that happened to them.

No wonder the garden of Eden came to represent the eternal bliss of living close to the Lord. In the Greek translation of the Hebrew Scripture during the third century BCE, the garden of Eden was called "paradise," which originally meant a royal garden. As used in the New Testament, "paradise" had come to mean eternal life in heaven.[25] Traditionally Jews called the hereafter either "the World to Come" or the "Garden of Eden."[26] In both Judaism and Christianity, the bliss of the ancient garden suggests the bliss to be found in the afterlife.

LIVING BY THE STORY

Rather than looking for a glorified future, I am more interested in what the garden of Eden tells us about the way life is best lived now. Hallmarks of the garden include a sacred quality of life with glimmers of bliss. From my memories of the farm, such happiness seems easier to find when family, work, and community are seamlessly integrated into a life centered on faith.

Research on religious involvement confirms its impact on happiness. After reviewing numerous studies, Robert D. Putnam, a professor emeritus of public policy at Harvard, and his colleague David E. Campbell, a political science professor at Notre Dame, concluded that religious involvement is one of the strongest predictors of life satisfaction.[27] Among the correlates of satisfaction in these studies, healthy people are happier than sick people, married people are happier than single people, and friends matter more than material possessions. Although money buys happiness for people living in poverty, it does not buy that much happiness after people reach a comfortable standard of living. Religious involvement is more powerful. Other things being equal, the difference in happiness between a non-churchgoer and a weekly churchgoer is more than the difference in happiness between someone making a low income and another person making ten times more money.

Religious people also tend to be more generous. In reviewing many surveys, Putnam and Campbell found that religious involvement repeatedly correlates with greater generosity.[28] In comparison with others with similar demographic characteristics, people who regularly attend religious services are much more likely to volunteer their services and donate their money to charitable causes. As expected, they give more time and money than others to religious causes. But this is only one form of their generosity. They also give more time and money than others to secular causes. While they support a wide range of secular causes, they are especially likely to help the young, elderly, and needy.

Taking a closer look, Putnam and Campbell found that attendance at religious services was not enough to explain life satisfaction and altruism. The professors attribute the happiness and generosity of religious people to friendships formed with other religious people through participating in religious activities and talking about religion with family and friends. Through this involvement, religious people build social networks of morally freighted personal connections, coupled with an inclination toward altruism. These moral, altruistic connections in turn reinforce a strong sense of religious identity. The professors use the term "supercharged" to describe religious friendships because of their powerful impact on life satisfaction and altruism.[29]

If we are not involved in religious organizations, we may still find ways to boost our happiness, but it takes more effort. Putnam and Campbell concede that a close, morally intense social network may have a strong impact on well-being even if it is not religious. They could not exclude this possibility because they were unable to find a significant number of such groups nationwide to study. They are confident that religious institutions are by far the most common locations of close, altruistic networks in this country.[30] Taking a different approach, Laurie Santos, a Yale psychology professor, acknowledges that religious people tend to be happier in the sense of life satisfaction and positive emotion in the moment. But she says people can find happiness by meditating, volunteering, and engaging in social connections without involvement in religious activities. Even so, she admits that structuring our lives this way is much easier if we are involved in religious organizations.[31]

My friend Elizabeth epitomizes to me a lifetime supercharged by relationships in religious organizations. Raised in a close-knit Italian family, she went to Catholic schools from first grade through college, and after she graduated, she continued going to Mass every week and staying involved in parish activities. As an adult, she realized that the heavenly bliss she had associated with the garden of Eden in her childhood could be found on earth. She glimpsed the garden's joy whenever she felt as though she were walking with Jesus. As she explained, "Eternal life is living in God's presence and comes to us whenever we experience the sacred." To her, the garden meant "happiness, everything that we want, what life is like when we live in God's image." In one of her most sacred moments, she felt God's presence in the room as soon as she and her husband saw the infant they adopted.

As suggested by Putnam and Campbell's studies, Elizabeth's life was characterized by generosity. Together with her church friends, she seemed to know everyone in the neighborhood who needed help. One day she would be taking an ill or disabled neighbor to a medical appointment. Another day she would be lining up social services for a frail and isolated woman who no longer could take care of herself. Saturday mornings were devoted to serving communion with a priest to patients at a local hospital.

When Elizabeth's daughter went to community college, Elizabeth invited her daughter's friends from Asia and Latin America to Thanksgiving dinners. Taking the place of a parent, Elizabeth attended the graduation ceremony of one student and took him out to dinner to celebrate. Struggling with economic hardship, the man later joined the US Army to pay for additional education and become a citizen. Elizabeth meant so much to him that he invited her to attend his graduation from boot camp and offered to pay her way with his hard-earned cash if she could not afford the trip.

If we are looking for a fulfilling life, I would choose the Bible before self-help books on happiness. Creation in God's image connects us to something greater than ourselves while the garden of Eden portrays the close ties that lead to intimacy and bliss. We may find many other ways to connect with something greater, strengthen our relationships, and enjoy a fulfilling life. But for Elizabeth, Matt, and my other relatives on the farm, the biblical stories suggest the blueprint that made their lives "almost perfect."

3

Darkness outside the Garden

How has the dark side of human nature affected you and others you know?
GENESIS 3:1–24 (EXILE FROM THE GARDEN OF EDEN);
4:1–16 (CAIN AND ABEL)

JUST BEFORE MY SOPHOMORE year in high school, I glared across the dinner table at my stepfather with sheer contempt. He had stopped offering back rubs years ago. But a week before that dinner, I had been sleeping in my bed when I woke up in the middle of the night, feeling his hands on my genitals. Too horrified to know what to do, I did nothing until it happened a second time. When he came home from work the next day and sat down to eat, I looked at him with total disdain, and after that, to my relief, he never did it again.

Telling my mother was out of the question. She had begun hitting me on my head with a hairbrush during her pregnancy with my half-sister. Then she became increasingly abusive when my stepfather lost the family savings in a failed start-up and, later, lost his job and remained unemployed for six months. As soon as I came home from school, she would yell at me in a rage, disparaging me while complaining she had nothing growing up and still had nothing. Moving closer, she would swing her arms to hit me while I shielded my face with my hands, the entire time backing up until I ended up in a corner. Then she would grab my arms with both of her hands, shaking me back and forth, carefully shifting her fingernails to avoid incriminating marks.

After Mom was too exhausted to hit me anymore, she usually collapsed onto her bed. Other times she threatened to kill herself in the bathroom or to take the car keys to drive away and never return. Around then, my stepfather would emerge from his hiding place in the basement. He told me, "If anything ever happens to your mother, you'll be kicked out of the house that day." I pictured myself standing alone on the street corner with my suitcase, relieved to be out of a hellhole, yet scared about what would happen next.

In early December of my sophomore year in high school, Mom took me to a discount store to try on an orange-and-yellow plaid suit. Even though I had told her I did not like it, when I opened my gift on Christmas Eve, there was the orange-and-yellow plaid suit. After I said nothing the rest of the evening, Mom remarked, "You've been awfully quiet." I responded, "You knew I didn't like that suit." Then she flew into another rage, saying she would never again buy any clothes for me. After that, I used money from babysitting and clerking in department stores to buy my own clothes and pay for my personal expenses.

Before my junior year of high school, my stepfather bought a bigger house well beyond his means to appease my mother for losing his job and their savings. Before we even moved in, Mom purchased on credit new furniture for every room, telling me, "Everything has always been for you, and now I want something for myself." Stuck in a house that felt less like a home than ever, I badly wanted to escape to college. But my mother and stepfather told me I could go to college only if I stayed with them and went to the state university. I finally found a way to leave for college and law school by working long hours at numerous jobs and living on virtually no money.

After I left, my mother and stepfather continued their financial shenanigans. Before I went to law school in New York City, I wanted to sell the car I had bought for my job in the Midwest. My stepfather insisted on buying my car because, he said, "I've never been able to give you money for college and this would be something I could do for you." Then he took the car and never paid me for it. When my grandparents found out, they told him they could pay me for the car out of their meager savings. But my stepfather asked them to give him the money because, he said, "I want to pay her myself." After they gave him the money, he pocketed it instead. Many years passed before my grandparents learned he had kept their money. They felt he had taken advantage of them because of their old age, but I knew he was a swindler at heart. To me, my entire relationship with both my mother and stepfather was a scam.

The story of Adam and Eve's expulsion from the garden of Eden helps to explain why I grew up in dread of my mother and stepfather. If Adam and Eve's story had ended in the garden's bliss, it would have left out the dark side of life that we experience. Outside the garden, people kill, rape, rob, injure, and defraud, and the innocent suffer from other people's greed and rage. By contrasting the strengths and weaknesses of human nature, the story helps us make sense of the vile events of life and find a way to cope.

THE BIBLE'S STORY

The Bible describes the dark side of human nature by Adam and Eve's expulsion from the garden to live as we do outside of Eden. Instead of enjoying the idyllic life in the garden, the couple ended up in a family torn apart by violence. Yet the story of Adam and Eve's family gives hope for mastering sin and restoring justice.

As told in Genesis 2:16–17, Yahweh protected Adam from evil by a single command: "You may freely eat of every tree of the garden, but of the tree of the knowledge of good and evil you shall not eat, for in the day that you eat of it you shall die." In the next chapter, a serpent, which is described as the craftiest of wild animals, questioned Eve about this command, telling her, "You will not die, for God knows that when you eat of it your eyes will be opened, and you will be like God, knowing good and evil."[32] Since Eve saw that the tree was good for food, a delight to the eyes, and desirable for wisdom, she ate its fruit and gave some to Adam. Then the eyes of both of them were opened, they realized they were naked, and they sewed fig leaves together and made loincloths to cover themselves.

Later they heard Yahweh walking in the garden in the evening breeze. When Yahweh asked Adam where he was, he admitted hiding because he was naked and afraid. The couple bore a heavy burden for having eaten the forbidden fruit. Yahweh told Eve he would increase her "pain" in childbearing, which perhaps is better translated as "multiply her toilsome pregnancies."[33] Instead of mutual desire and cooperation, she would desire her husband, and he would rule over her. Yahweh told Adam that the ground was cursed because of him, and he would toil for his food all the days of his life. Hard labor, debilitating pregnancies, and male rule were certainly far different from the life envisioned by God in the garden of

Eden. As biblical scholar Phyllis Trible points out, these conditions resulted from the disintegration of the bond Adam and Eve had with the creator, nature, and each other.[34]

Afterward Adam named his wife Eve (a word resembling "living" in Hebrew) because she was the mother of all living, and Yahweh clothed the couple in leather garments indicative of civilization.[35] Then Yahweh made a startling observation in Genesis 3:22: Now that Adam and Eve had eaten from the tree of knowledge of good and evil, they had become like divine beings, "knowing good and evil," and if they stayed in the garden, they might also eat from another tree called the tree of life and live forever. To stop them from eating from the tree of life and living forever, Yahweh drove them out of the garden to till the ground elsewhere.

In other words, Yahweh allowed Adam and Eve to make their own choices even if their choices were contrary to Yahweh's command. When making an independent decision, they violated the prohibition against eating from the tree of knowledge of good and evil. Now that they had such knowledge, they might choose evil over good again and again. Given this propensity for evil, Yahweh did not want them to live forever and become an immortal adversary.[36]

After Adam and Eve left the garden, their family life went dreadfully awry. As told in Genesis 4, their son Cain was a farmer who offered some produce to Yahweh, while their son Abel was a shepherd who offered the firstborn of his flock. Although the story says Yahweh had more regard for Abel and his offering, it does not explain why and focuses instead on Cain's reaction to God's rebuff.[37] When Cain became angry, Yahweh told him, "If you do well, will you not be accepted? And if you do not do well, sin is lurking at the door; its desire is for you, but you must master it."[38] This is the first mention of sin in the Bible. Sin seems to be an internal inclination personified as a ravenous beast or demon, which an individual can and must control. With moral and psychological insight, the passage suggests that dark instincts made Cain more vulnerable to sin when things did not work out as desired, but the passage still requires him to take personal responsibility. Despite dark instincts, we can make good choices.[39]

Rather than heeding this advice, Cain invited his brother Abel to go into the field. There Cain rose up against his brother and killed him. Afterward, as told in Genesis 4:9, Yahweh asked Cain, "Where is your brother Abel?" And Cain replied, "I do not know; am I my brother's keeper?" From the rest of the Bible, we know the answer is yes.

God's reaction to the murder was swift. Yahweh said that Abel's blood was crying from the ground, which would no longer yield to Cain's cultivation. Cain pleaded that this punishment would be more than he could bear, he would be a fugitive and wanderer, and anyone he met could kill him. In an act of mercy, Yahweh put a mark on him so he would not be killed. Then Cain left the divine presence and settled in a land east of Eden.

Since I had longed for someone to restrain my own family's misconduct, I took comfort in God's punishment of Cain's crime. In place of courts and police, the Lord spoke on the victim's behalf, punished the offender, and restored justice to the community. Any mercy toward Cain did not undercut the story's message to master sinful impulses and protect one another. Each of us is our brother's (and sister's) keeper.

WRITING THE STORY

Adam and Eve's story combined many historical trends to suggest the strengths and limitations of human nature. The story was not intended as a philosophical treatise on free will, morality, or death. It reflects instead life as it was experienced by the people writing, adapting, compiling, and interpreting the text, and their experiences still resonate with us today.

An early version of Adam and Eve's story reflects the Mesopotamian notion that education leads to humanity. Long before the Israelite monarchy, a student in ancient Sumer had told his teacher: "You have opened my eyes as though I were a puppy; you have formed humanity within me."[40] These words are mirrored in the words of our story about Adam and Eve. As described in Genesis 3:7, after they ate from the tree of knowledge of good and evil, "the eyes of both were opened" like the eyes of the Sumerian student. Wisdom is emphasized by the snake symbolizing wisdom and the tree of knowledge symbolizing wisdom's fruit. From this perspective, the narrative is a coming-of-age story in which Adam and Eve gain the wisdom to be fully human.[41]

Like the characters in Mesopotamian legends, after Adam and Eve acquired wisdom, they were forced out of their harmonious life in the garden of Eden. In the Gilgamesh epic, Enkidu faced a similar consequence. Formed from clay like Adam, Enkidu lived at first a free and peaceful life in harmony with nature. But once the wise woman helped him become wise and human, his unity with nature was broken, the animals no longer ran with him, and he left for a more civilized world represented by the city. In the biblical story, Eve, like the wise woman, helped to open Adam's eyes to wisdom, after which he left the garden of Eden for a settled agricultural life.[42]

In another similarity to Mesopotamian literature, Adam and Eve lost the chance to live forever once they acquired wisdom. In the Gilgamesh epic, wisdom went along with death as part of the human condition. Heartbroken over Enkidu's death, Gilgamesh searched for immortality and found a plant to make himself immortal. But a snake ate it first, allowing it to shed its skin to keep rejuvenating itself. Finally content with mortal status, Gilgamesh appreciated the benefits of civilization found in the fine buildings, quarries, gardens, and pastures of the city where he was the king.[43]

Instead of royal privileges in an urban setting, civilization in Adam and Eve's story led to the harsh conditions of Israel's agricultural society. While agriculture enabled more stable food supplies and family relations, men endured hard labor, toiling in the fields, and women had many pregnancies marred by high infant and maternal mortality. The Israelites also lacked adequate protection from violent encounters. Even though Cain's story may have initially explained why a particular tribe known as the Kenites had such fierce warriors, the story later resonated with the Israelites' experience of violence well beyond this tribe.[44]

From around 300 BCE to 200 CE, first Jewish and later Christian sages revamped their understanding of Adam and Eve's story along with the rest of Hebrew Scripture.[45] They saw the story as a morality tale about opposing poles of good and evil. Adam and Eve could have obeyed God and lived forever in bliss. But they had been tempted by a snake now identified as Satan, their disobedience had brought sin into the world, and they had lost the chance to live forever in the garden. Outside the garden, Cain and Abel portrayed the struggle of good with evil while Cain's banishment encouraged others to choose God's side.[46]

Both Judaism and Christianity found ways to reconcile us with God despite our sinful tendencies. In Judaism, Adam and Eve's disobedience showed an innate desire for evil that could be overcome by the Torah's divine teachings. According to the rabbis, the human heart is divided between an inclination to good and an inclination to evil. Besides loving God with the good inclination, we need to convert the evil inclination to love God too. In the rabbis' view, the practice and study of the Torah renews intimacy with God and leads to eternal life.[47] In Christianity, Adam and Eve's disobedience, known as the "fall," corrupted human nature and requires God's grace to overcome. As explained in the New Testament, Adam introduced the old creation to sin, which in turn led to death, while Christ became the savior of the new creation, reconciling a broken world and offering eternal life.[48]

The profound significance of Judeo-Christian views of intimacy, estrangement, and reconciliation with the divine was obscured when Augustine, a North African theologian, used the term "original sin" in the year 396 CE.[49] In his view, human nature was created in a sound state, but corrupted by sin tainting every aspect of existence and not easily controlled. In a sermon given in the year 419 CE, he suggested that sex passed down original sin from one generation to the next. But Christ could save us because he had been conceived without sex by a virgin mother. Pointing to Adam and Eve covering their bodies with fig leaves in the garden of Eden, Augustine proclaimed:

> What they covered up is where they felt shame. There you have what original sin is derived from, there you have the reason why nobody is born without sin. There you have the reason why the Lord did not wish to be so conceived, the Lord whom the virgin conceived. He broke the hold of sin, because he came without it; he broke its hold because he did not come from it.[50]

In the same era, Judaism developed its own version of original sin. Around 500 CE, the Talmud, a central text of rabbinic Judaism, recounted: "When the serpent copulated with Eve, he imposed pollution in her." The pollution of the serpent led to the notion that the first sin was transmitted from Adam and Eve to their descendants and that the Torah's divine law would overcome the serpent's pollution.[51]

To compensate for the lurid aspects of original sin, many modern theologians emphasize personal responsibility for conduct along with the joy of sex. They do not view Adam and Eve's story as a historical event that changed people from good to bad. Neither do they look at Adam and Eve as genetic forebears of sin. Rather, they find in the fall a fundamental truth about our enormous potential and dismal failures. Although we could choose a joyful life as portrayed in the garden of Eden, we often yield to our baser motives and bring down others with us. Adam and Eve's story is an imaginative portrayal of the destructive tendencies that affect our personal lives, families, communities, and global affairs.[52]

LIVING BY THE STORY

The updated view of the fall rings true to my experience. My mother and stepfather could have chosen to conduct themselves with decency and constrain their baser motives. Instead, they let their emotions get out of hand and reinforced each other's vile behavior. The deeper they sank, the more they tried to take me down with them. If, as Putnam and Campbell found, religious friendships are supercharged for happiness, toxic relationships are supercharged for misery.

Harvard psychologist Steven Pinker provides a practical explanation of Cain's rage.[53] In his view, human nature is characterized by what he calls better angels and inner demons. Better angels include empathy, self-control, reason, and to some extent, moral sense, and inner demons include greed, dominance, revenge, sadism, and some ideologies. Although Pinker relates the angels and demons to components of our brains, he finds that personal circumstances and social forces influence whether the angels or the demons get the upper hand. Over time, the expansion of government, courts, police, and commercial trade has greatly reduced murders outside the family. While the killing of children, parents, spouses, and siblings is less common, the rate of such murders declines more slowly, perhaps because of deeply rooted conflicts of interest. Even so, domestic violence and abuse have decreased due to changing norms, humanitarian reforms, and intervention by police and social service agencies.

Pinker's analysis seems to support some aspects of both Jewish and Christian views. The better angels and inner demons are a lot like the tendency toward good and the tendency toward evil in Jewish lore. But we do not choose between these impulses in a vacuum. As Pinker observes, we are influenced by our cultural norms, communities, and living situations. Considering the fall, many Christians believe these conditions can be quagmires compounding bad choices. In any case, the reduction in violence and abuse documented by Pinker suggests ways we can act as our brother's keeper by protecting people from attacks and helping perpetrators control their dark side.

To overcome inner demons, my Jewish friend Dan counted on willpower. Thrilled to be made in God's image, he was baffled by the garden of Eden story, saying, "Why would God exclude knowledge of good and evil?" Cain's story reinforced his view that everyone has an innate tendency to do good and an innate tendency to do evil and that the evil tendency can be overcome by an act of will. He insisted, "People need to rise above their circumstances. We can't excuse wrongdoing."

From a lifetime of supercharged relationships, my Catholic friend Elizabeth had learned that spiritual restoration helps to remake us in God's image. She considered Adam and Eve representative of each of us and our destructive tendencies. As she explained, "Although we could have a close relationship with God, we put ourselves in God's place and let things go askew." But she did not think we should lose hope: "When we once again appreciate the sacred quality of our existence, we can experience eternal life even now in the midst of our daily activities." As she put it, "We're not just made in God's image; we're also restored to God's image."

Given my family's turmoil, I would advocate for more government and community organizations to help us act as our brother's keeper. As Dan suggested, when we struggle to do the right thing, we can use our willpower just as God urged Cain to do. We may also find, like Elizabeth did, that faith helps us make better choices. But neither our personal choices nor our personal faith is enough to protect us from the destructive conduct of others. When Abel's blood cries out from the ground, Abel represents the blameless victims of all the people who have not controlled their inner demons. If we are truly our brother's keeper, we should provide courts, policing, and community resources to reduce violence both inside and outside the home. To the extent we give the angels an edge over the demons, fewer people would live in conditions supercharged for misery.

4

Justice and Compassion in Noah's Flood

When faced with wrongdoing, do you restore justice by correcting the wrong, or do you show compassion by forgiving the offender?

EXCERPTS FROM GENESIS 6:5—9:29 IN APPENDIX D

WHILE GROWING UP, I never understood why pastors kept talking about forgiveness when I had more pressing problems—my parents were hitting, molesting, and stealing from me. Even worse, our local church seemed to support my parents' misconduct. My mother became increasingly abusive the entire time she went to therapy at the church's mental health service. Instead of helping me, the pastors and Sunday school teachers told children to obey their parents, never asking children how they were treated at home or teaching them to protect themselves. Like many abusers, my parents warned me against telling anyone outside the home what happened in the family, and by stressing obedience, the church reinforced their warning. I felt I had nowhere to turn.

To explain my family's dynamics, a psychiatrist told me many years later that Mom never thought of me as her child. Consequently, she expected Grandma to do much of the childcare, and that put Grandma in the role of a mother to both Mom and me. Late in life, with a sense of wonder, Grandma even said to me, "Sometimes you seem more like my child than my grandchild." But having the same mother did not make me

JUSTICE AND COMPASSION IN NOAH'S FLOOD

Mom's sister. We were more like stepsisters because we had different dads. The psychiatrist interpreted Mom's behavior as that of a jealous stepsister who wanted me to fail.

I appreciate the story of Noah and the flood because it provides a more balanced approach to the world's cruelty than my childhood pastors suggested. In the story, human wickedness was so pervasive that God destroyed the world and started all over again. By the end of the story, God realized that human inclinations were still evil, but accepted people anyway. Yet the story clarifies that unconditional divine love does not mean approving of misconduct or enduring violence and abuse. God remained the majestic and powerful creator who made us in his image and urges us to live up to our potential.

Both dimensions of the creator are crucial to our understanding of God. When I have talked with people who felt unloved or unlovable, they have told me how much God's unconditional love has meant for turning around their lives. But I never felt unlovable, because I always knew my grandparents loved me and they told me Jesus loves me too. Much more upsetting to me was letting my parents get by with blatant wrongs. By presenting both dimensions of the creator, the flood story suggests that we can be held to a higher standard of conduct even though we are forgiven for our shortcomings.

THE BIBLE'S STORY

The Israelites dramatized the tension between justice and compassion when they portrayed the destruction of the world's wickedness in a flood. This tension is most apparent if we separate the parts of the story written by the scribes from the parts written by the priests. If you read about the flood in Genesis 6:5—9:29, you can see how the stories of the scribes and priests have been combined in the Bible. The separate versions of the scribes and priests are set forth in appendix D and described below.[54]

The scribes had described the tragic consequences of sin when writing about Adam and Eve's family. In Genesis 6:5 of the scribes' flood story, Yahweh "saw that the wickedness of humans was great in the earth and that every inclination of the thoughts of their hearts was only evil continually." He was so grieved in his heart that he regretted making them and decided to blot them out in a flood.

Even so, Noah found favor with the Lord. Yahweh told him to board an ark with his family, along with one pair of every kind of animal, plus additional animals for sacrifices. After Noah's household went into the ark, Yahweh personally shut the door and brought on forty days of rain. Except for Noah's entourage, every living thing was wiped out.

After the rain stopped, Noah sent a dove out several times to look for dry land. When the dove did not return, Noah knew it had found dry land. He left the ark and made a sacrifice to Yahweh. Smelling its pleasing odor, Yahweh had a change of heart and promised never again to destroy every living creature.

Although Yahweh realized people were still drawn to evil, he accepted them anyway. Recalling the curse upon Adam and Eve when leaving the garden of Eden, Yahweh said: "I will never again curse the ground because of humans, for the inclination of the human heart is evil from youth"; and Yahweh promised continuous agricultural cycles regardless of human shortcomings: "As long as the earth endures, / seedtime and harvest, cold and heat, / summer and winter, day and night shall not cease."[55]

The scribes' story of unconditional love suggests the point made by my pastors. God never gives up on us. The Lord does not say we will be accepted only if we start doing better. We can be accepted just as we are.

Even so, the priests' version of the flood story clarifies that divine love does not mean approving of misconduct or enduring violence and abuse. When the priests wrote the creation story at the beginning of the Bible, they emphasized God's intent for a righteous world. In Genesis 6:12–13 of the priests' flood story, God saw that "the earth was corrupt, for all flesh had corrupted its ways upon the earth" and "the earth is filled with violence because of them." Consequently, God destroyed all flesh along with the earth except for Noah's entourage, and then God provided a fresh start so that people can live as intended in God's image. To convey this message, the priests' version emphasized Noah's upright character and God's concern for Noah's life.[56]

In the priests' account, God's concern for Noah was the turning point in the flood. After the Lord saw the earth had become corrupt and filled with violence, it was returned to primordial watery chaos. The fountains of the deep burst forth, the windows of the heavens were opened, and waters swelled for 150 days. Then God remembered Noah. After that, the Lord blew a wind over the earth like the wind that blew over watery chaos at creation. The water subsided as the fountains of the deep and the windows of heaven were closed.

In the priests' version of the flood, just as God had done at the beginning of creation, God blessed Noah and his family and commanded them to be fruitful and multiply and fill the earth. Considering the world's violent past, God warned of a reckoning for any person who takes another's life. By way of explanation, God reasserted that "in his own image / God made humans."[57] Then God promised Noah, his descendants, and every living creature that a flood would never again destroy the earth, and as a sign of this promise, God put a rainbow in the sky.

God's concern for righteousness was the kind of assurance I wanted from my pastors. No one should be mistreated by other people. When a child, spouse, or disabled or elderly individual suffers abuse, or anyone endures violence or injustice, the creator holds the perpetrator to a moral standard.

WRITING THE STORY

Hundreds of years before the biblical writings about a flood, the Atrahasis epic in Mesopotamia described a great flood, and a version of that story was included in the Gilgamesh epic.[58] In a land prone to floods, the story explained that the Mesopotamian gods decided to destroy people with a flood because of overpopulation and noise. But one god tipped off the man who later built an ark and survived in it with his household and animals. Like the biblical story, in the Gilgamesh epic, the man sent out a dove and other birds to search for dry land, and once the ark reached dry land, the man made a sacrifice to the gods, and smelling the pleasing odor, the gods decided against killing people with another flood.

Along with Adam and Eve's story, the flood story by the Israelite scribes may date as far back as the monarchy of Solomon.[59] Although the scribes seem to have been influenced by the Mesopotamian flood story, they recast the story to express their own concerns. They lived in a highland area that was not prone to floods, and they were not interested in overpopulation and noise. Instead of describing a conflict among the gods, the scribes' version as told in the Bible portrays how Yahweh intended to destroy people because of their wickedness but then changed his mind despite their evil inclinations.

Several centuries later, while the Israelites were living in exile in Babylon, the scribes undertook a major literary project to make sense of Jerusalem's destruction, and in the absence of a monarchy, their narrative referred to elders who were prominent lay leaders during and after the exile. In writing the narrative, the scribes wanted to understand why the Israelites had suffered such catastrophic losses and how they could find a better way forward. To do so, they compiled, revised, and expanded texts that scribes had previously written, including the stories about Adam and Eve and the flood. Then they appeared to produce a sweeping narrative beginning with Adam and Eve and the flood, continuing with Abraham and his progeny, and concluding with Moses leading the Israelites out of Egypt to Israel.[60]

The Israelite priests remained another prominent group during and after the exile. In response to the scribes' narrative, the priests seemed to compile their own narrative with their own point of view. Their account began with creation in God's image, continued with the restoration of creation after the flood, and concluded with God's creation of the holy community of Israel. In their account, the flood story did not include sacrifices and additional animals for sacrifices because God had not yet provided instructions for the involvement of priests in sacrifices.[61]

After a Persian king conquered Babylon in 539 BCE, some exiles returned to Jerusalem to rebuild the city. When the Persians conquered territories, they tended to support the local gods, laws, and leaders of the conquered people. That way the Persians could more easily control the local population, and the local leaders could gain more authority with Persian support. In line with this approach, the Persians encouraged Israelite exiles in Babylon to rebuild Jerusalem and its temple and may have influenced the development of the Torah read by the Israelite Ezra in the biblical account.[62]

As the Bible reports, after the completion of the new temple in Jerusalem, the Persian king commissioned Ezra, an exile living in Babylon, to check whether the Israelites in Jerusalem were obeying "the law of [Ezra's] God and the law of the king."[63] At that time, the elders in Jerusalem may have been supporting the narrative written by scribes, and the priests in the city may have been supporting the narrative written by priests. Since competing narratives would not have been conducive to unified rule of the city, Ezra may have encouraged combining these narratives into a single text much like the first five books of the Bible today. That way he could present the text as the Hebrew law that was authorized by the Persian king and required the Israelites' obedience. Even though we cannot be certain of when and why the narratives were combined, the biblical account tells us that Ezra read a text to the Israelites in a grand public ceremony, and the text seems to have been the combined narrative of the scribes and priests. Known as the Torah or law of Moses, it became a central text of the Jewish community down to the present day.[64]

When integrating the work of the scribes and priests, the Israelite editors preserved the perspective of both groups. The editors sometimes put the two versions side by side, as we see with the priests' creation story followed by the scribes' story of the garden of Eden. In the case of the flood, however, the two accounts were combined into a single narrative, most likely because of God's promise never again to repeat the catastrophe.[65]

In combining the work of both the scribes and the priests, the Israelite editors took a different approach than we would take today. Now we value consistency, avoid repetition, and prefer a uniform style. Back then, the Israelite editors had so much respect for the work of both the scribes and priests that their material was left intact as much as possible. As a result, the combined flood story is sometimes inconsistent and repetitious with different styles and terms. But the Israelite editors succeeded in achieving their more important goal of preserving the perspective of both groups.

By presenting the views of both the scribes and priests, the Bible provides a deeper understanding of our potential and limitations. During the Middle Ages, the rabbis explained why God would balance compassion with justice:

> A king had some empty glasses. He said, "If I pour hot water into them, they will crack; if I pour ice-cold water into them they will also crack!" What did the king do? He mixed the hot and the cold water together and poured it into them and they did not crack. Even so did the Holy One, blessed be He, say, "If I create the world on the basis of the attribute of mercy alone, the world's sins will greatly multiply. If I create it on the basis of the attribute of justice alone, how could the world endure? I will therefore create it with both the attributes of mercy and justice, and may it endure!"[66]

The need to balance mercy with justice was missing from the sermons I heard during my childhood as I remember them. Too much emphasis on love, forgiveness, and obedience may exacerbate the problems of troubled families and communities. Focusing on education and mental health has serious limitations too. Violence and abuse may be better resolved by enforcing laws against the perpetrators and providing safer living situations for their victims.

LIVING BY THE STORY

When we contrast the views of the scribes and priests, the flood story seems much more relevant to our lives today. Like the scribes, we may believe God accepts us even though we are drawn to destructive acts, and like the priests, we may feel God wants us to live as people made in God's image. When faced with wrongdoing, we can consider the way the story balances forgiveness with higher expectations.

Although we do not know what kind of wickedness, violence, and corruption disturbed God in the flood story, we know a great deal about the world's atrocities in subsequent historical periods. Matthew White, an American librarian with a passion for researching tragedies, considered the enormity of some of these atrocities. He estimated sixteen million deaths from capture to settlement of Africans in the Atlantic slave trade during the fifteenth to nineteenth centuries, fifteen million deaths beginning in 1492 from violence and disease annihilating American Indians, and fifteen million deaths of soldiers and civilians in World War I, followed by sixty-six million in World War II.[67] When Harvard professor Steven Pinker analyzed White's data in proportion to the world's population, Pinker considered one of the worst catastrophes to be forty million deaths in the Mongol conquests led by Genghis Khan during the thirteenth century.[68]

Considering atrocities of this magnitude, we may find it easier to understand the impulse to destroy the world's wickedness in a flood and start all over again. But human weakness is so great that many people would be condemned as perpetrators of injustice, and even if we start all over, human nature will result in more injustices. The flood story can be read as a metaphor that illustrates the tension between treating wrongdoers with compassion and making things right.

When I talked about the flood story with my friends, their personal experiences predisposed them one way or another toward justice or mercy. While Ben attended a Jewish school as a child, he was, he said, "too busy learning Hebrew to worry about the morality of the flood." But he still learned the values central to his faith. By the time he grew up, he credited his upbringing with instilling a passion for social justice. When he reconsidered the flood story as an adult, he called God "the good sheriff in the Wild West," restoring order in a lawless community.

Siding with mercy, Hannah was influenced by an affair with a married man that was exacerbated by her struggles with alcohol abuse. After growing up in a Protestant home, she dropped out of church when the unfortunate affair wracked her with guilt and the church intensified her shame. She said, "The fall and flood story are about sin and judgment, and that's what gives religion a bad name." In her view, people mean well and do the best they can but succumb to human weakness. She said, "We keep falling down and need to keep picking ourselves back up and always deserve another chance."

For many parents, teaching their children responsibility while forgiving their lapses is a familiar dilemma. Although parents want to give their children unconditional love and spare them damaging repercussions, parents also want their children to understand the seriousness of their behavior and face its consequences. Deciding the right balance is especially heart-wrenching when teenagers and adult children engage in irresponsible, self-destructive, or criminal conduct, sometimes made worse by mental illness or substance abuse. In these situations, I know parents who make excruciating decisions about whether to call the police to intervene; whether to pay for bail, lawyers, and counseling services; and whether to keep paying for them as their children's problems continue.

I appreciate the way the flood story finds a balance between divine acceptance despite our baser inclinations and divine encouragement to live up to moral standards despite our past failures. Of course, most of us would prefer justice when we are wronged and compassion when we are in the wrong, and to be honest, we often take injustices that we suffer more seriously than injustices we commit. If we are too quick to forgive, the offenders may never fully repent, their misconduct may continue, and victims will lack protection and redress. If we never forgive, we sometimes end up so bitter we cannot move on with life. In contrast to the one-sided sermons I heard about forgiveness, the scribes and priests writing the flood story remind us to balance compassion with justice.

PART II

Taking a Journey

(Second Part of Genesis)

5

Abraham Counting the Stars

What inspires you to change direction at major turning points in your life?

GENESIS 12:1–5 (GOD'S CALL); 15:1–6 (COUNTING THE STARS); 16:1–16 (HAGAR FLEEING HARSH TREATMENT); 18:1–15 (DIVINE VISIT WITH ABRAHAM AND SARAH); 21:8–21 (HAGAR AND HER SON CAST OUT)

MY DENTIST WAS CHECKING my teeth for cavities when he gave me one of the best tips for my future. At the time, I wanted nothing more than to leave home for college, but the high school teachers in my working-class suburb knew little about higher education. The principal and senior teachers had gone to college for only two years, the students tied for the lowest college attendance in the Minneapolis area, and those continuing their education typically went to the state university near their homes. As an outsider from the East Coast, my dentist suggested Carleton College in Northfield, Minnesota, calling it the Harvard of the Midwest. After hearing his advice, I applied to Carleton and was delighted to be admitted.

When I went to college, I soon learned that most of my fellow students came from prosperous families and had gone to academically superior high schools. Although I had been aware of social class differences, I had not realized the vast extent to which selective colleges cater to the well off and provide credentials, contacts, and know-how for more promising careers. I felt that I was part of a new world with much better odds for success.

After graduating from college, I went to law school at New York University in New York City. As the law school grew from a regional institution to national prominence, it championed a greater percentage of women in law and became a gateway to high-quality work at top law firms. From an improbable background, I sought to mirror my upstart school by breaking into a male profession in a world-renowned city.

As my legal career advanced, I became a partner at several large law firms. Representing companies involved in financings and acquisitions seemed a natural fit. I relished the challenge of working on innovative business arrangements, I enjoyed negotiating contracts on terms that protected my client's interests, and I liked writing descriptions of a company's strengths and weaknesses for investors buying its securities. On every deal, it was exciting to work with business executives and their investment bankers, lawyers, and accountants. The work seemed to soothe the wounds left by my parents' financial missteps and deception.

Long after I left my family for New York City, I pondered God's call to Abraham to leave behind his father's house for the promised land. His story made me wonder whether the same spiritual force that led him to the promised land had guided me from a troubled home to a better life. In a scene that captures the endless possibilities of Abraham's journey, the Lord told him that his descendants would be as numerous as the stars. To this day, he is considered the father of Jews, Christians, and Muslims. His story has inspired many people in varying circumstances to find a more fulfilling life.

THE BIBLE'S STORY

After the creation and flood stories, beginning in Genesis 11:27, the book focuses on Abraham and his progeny. As told in the Bible, Abraham and his family originally lived in southern Mesopotamia, where they worshiped local gods.[69] Instead of staying in what became the much-hated Babylonian empire, his father took him (then called Abram), his wife, Sarah (then called Sarai), and his nephew Lot to go to the land of Canaan. As described in Genesis 12:1–2, after they settled in a city partway there, God called Abraham to continue the journey: "Go from your country and your kindred and your father's house to the land that I will show you"; and upon the fulfillment of this command, the Lord would treat him like royalty: "I will make of you a great nation, and I will bless you and make your name great, so that you will be a blessing." A nation implied numerous people and political independence; a great name meant fame; and blessings suggested offspring, flocks, and other riches for Abraham and those associated with him.[70]

In response to God's call, Abraham traveled to Canaan with Sarah and Lot. Then seventy-five years old and childless, Abraham soon became rich in livestock, silver, and gold, but had difficulty getting his wife pregnant. When God told him yet again that the land would be given to him and his descendants, he reminded the Lord that he still had no children. Undaunted, in Genesis 15:5, God brought him outside and said: "Look toward heaven and count the stars, if you are able to count them.... So shall your descendants be." In response, Abraham believed the Lord, and the Lord considered him righteous. To ancient Israelites, Abraham's response did not mean believing despite the evidence. It meant profound trust in a personal God.[71]

Still, Abraham did not count on Sarah's fertility to fulfill God's promise. By ancient custom comparable to surrogate motherhood today, a wife could give her maid to her husband and claim the child as her own. In accordance with this custom, Sarah gave her Egyptian slave girl, Hagar, to her husband. As often translated in Genesis 16:5–6, after Hagar became pregnant with Abraham's child, she looked with "contempt" at Sarah, then Sarah "dealt harshly" with Hagar, and Hagar ran away from her. But the Hebrew verb translated as contempt means "to treat lightly." Instead of disdain, it implies that Hagar no longer looked up to Sarah with the deference expected of a slave. The Hebrew word for Sarah's behavior means "oppress." The Bible uses the same word to describe the way the Egyptians treated their Hebrew slaves before God saved them in the exodus.[72]

Appearing as an angel, God found Hagar near a spring in the wilderness. The angel asked where she was coming from and where she was going. When she said she was running away, the angel told her to return to her mistress and assured her of a promising future with a multitude of offspring. The angel told Hagar to call her future son Ishmael, meaning "God hears," for "the Lord has given heed to your affliction"; and realizing that the Lord was speaking to her, Hagar called the Lord "El-roi," which means "God of seeing" or "God who sees," for coming to her aid.[73] Then she returned to Abraham's household and bore Ishmael.

In Genesis 17, when Abraham was ninety-nine, God clarified the family's status in a sacred agreement called a covenant. By this agreement, Abraham would be the ancestor of kings, and Sarah would bear a son called

Isaac, who would be a child of the covenant. To reflect the couple's enhanced status, God changed their names from Abram to Abraham, which meant "ancestor of a multitude," and from Sarai to Sarah, meaning "princess."[74] As a sign of the covenant, Abraham circumcised all the men in his household, including his son, Ishmael. While Isaac would be the forefather of Israel, Ishmael would be the forefather of another great nation.

Later, in Genesis 18:1–15, the Lord appeared to Abraham by some oak trees as Abraham sat at the entrance to his tent in the heat of the day. When he looked up, he saw three men, but as the story unfolds, they seemed to be God with two angels.[75] In accord with ancient Near Eastern hospitality, even though Abraham was unaware of their divine nature, he ran to meet them, bowed down to the ground, and suggested they rest under a tree. When they agreed, he immediately selected a calf, asked his servant to prepare it, and told his wife to knead some flour for cakes. Then he set curds, milk, and meat before his guests and stood by them as they ate.

When the visitors asked about Sarah, Abraham told them that she was in the tent, and one of the visitors said that he would return when her son was born. Given the couple's advanced age and infertility struggles, Abraham previously had laughed when God had told him that Sarah would have a child. Now Sarah also laughed. In response, in Genesis 18:14, the Lord, who is clearly identified at this point in the text, asked a key question about divine power to change people's lives and world events: "Is anything too wonderful for the LORD? At the set time I will return to you, in due season, and Sarah shall have a son."

In Genesis 21:1–7, when Abraham was one hundred years old and Sarah was ninety, Sarah had the son promised by the Lord. As God had instructed, the boy was named Isaac, which means "he [God] laughs."[76] Sarah laughed with joy that she had given birth in old age. Her laughter expressed delight in the impossible odds that God had overcome.

After Sarah gave birth to Isaac, in Genesis 21:9, she saw Ishmael playing with her son. Literally translated, the text says that Ishmael was "making Isaac laugh," bringing out the characteristic for which he was named.[77] Sarah became so agitated that she told Abraham in Genesis 21:10: "Cast out this slave woman with her son, for the son of this slave woman shall not inherit along with my son Isaac." Despite Abraham's distress over this request, God told him to go along with Sarah's request because his name would be carried by Isaac's offspring. As additional comfort, God would make Ishmael's descendants into another nation because Ishmael was also Abraham's offspring.

Early the next morning, in Genesis 21:14–21, Abraham put the boy on Hagar's shoulders along with bread and a skin of water and sent them away. They wandered in the wilderness until their water was gone. Then Hagar cast the child under a bush and sat down a good distance away for she did not want to watch him die. As she wept, God heard the boy's voice, and an angel called to Hagar from heaven. When God opened her eyes, she saw a well of water and gave the boy a drink. As the boy grew up in the Lord's presence, he lived in the wilderness, became an expert with his bow, and married an Egyptian woman introduced by his mother.

After Sarah died, Abraham married an Arab woman named Keturah, who was really Hagar according to Jewish legend.[78] When Abraham died, both of his sons, Isaac and Ishmael, buried him near Sarah's grave.

For a couple thousand years, these vignettes about Abraham's family have been among the most cherished stories in the Bible. Jews took comfort in God's promise of a homeland, Christians were inspired by Abraham's trust in God, and Muslims found assurance that God cared about them too. If we are struggling to leave the past behind, or fleeing harsh treatment, or living in dire circumstances, or longing for a child, the stories offer hope. The narrative vividly portrays how God intervenes to improve the lives of people in difficult situations.

WRITING THE STORY

When we look at the origins of Abraham's narrative, we can see why it would offer hope.[79] Stories about Abraham were passed along by word of mouth for many centuries, perhaps as far back as the tribal period prior to the Israelite monarchy. During the Babylonian exile, the Israelite scribes expanded the stories to offer encouragement to the exiles, and the Israelite priests supplemented these efforts. Throughout the ages, the stories have been treasured for their ancient portrayal of intimacy with the divine along with their exilic promise of a better future. While conveying a common bond, the stories address the special needs of Jewish, Christian, and Muslim communities.

Indicative of the antiquity of the stories, the encounters of Abraham, Sarah, and Hagar with the divine suggest what is sometimes called the God of Old.[80] As explained by Harvard emeritus professor James Kugel, just as we think of God now, the God of Old had the power to do and control things that people cannot. But the God of Old was not all-knowing. He walked around, inspected, questioned, and tested the situation to find out what was happening. Neither was the God of Old present everywhere at once as we expect God to be today. He had a physical presence in some ways like an actual body. He usually stayed out of view behind an invisible curtain that divides ordinary from extraordinary reality, and he occasionally intervened in a manner that people could see or experience.

When the God of Old appeared in the biblical stories, he sometimes sent what appeared to be an angel or human being as an intermediary to talk to a person. At first, the person might realize that the human being is really an angel, and then it would no longer be the angel speaking but God himself. Suddenly the person hears what God was saying and grasps that it is true. In line with this pattern, Abraham perceived three men who were later identified as God with two angels, and Hagar perceived an angel whom she eventually realized was God.

During the Babylonian exile, Israelite scribes included encounters with the God of Old in a narrative to inspire the Israelites during one of the most devastating periods of their history. Jerusalem and its temple had been destroyed, their monarchy had fallen, and they had no land or country to call their own. Like other displaced communities living as a minority in another culture, the Israelites exiled in Babylon emphasized family traditions and regarded ancient ancestors as if they were royalty. Instead of focusing on their defeated monarchy, they recalled the close relationship of God with their ancestor Abraham, and they gave him the exalted status of a king. Before Jerusalem's destruction, the Israelites had said their king would be famous, and nations would be blessed in him. Now that the monarchy had fallen, these accolades were given to Abraham.[81]

To the Israelites exiled in Babylon, Abraham was much more than an esteemed ancestor. Their scribes reminded the exiles that God had promised the land of Israel to Abraham and his descendants, and the Israelite priests added a covenant between God and the Israelites signified by circumcision. The stories recalled how Abraham had once lived in the same area where the exiles were living, then he had left his home and country for the land God had promised, and afterward Israel had become a great nation. Even though Jerusalem was later destroyed by the Babylonians, God would bring the exiles back to Israel, and it would once again become a great nation. As demonstrated by Isaac's birth, nothing was impossible for the Lord.[82]

These stories about Abraham reinforced the message of the biblical prophets that God would redeem the exiles and return them to their homeland. Before the exile, the prophets had warned the Israelites that their sins might lead to the destruction of their country. Now that their country had been destroyed and they were living in despair, the prophets told them their suffering would end. Even if their situation seemed hopeless, they could count on God's promise to their ancestors and God's power to overcome any obstacles.[83]

Given God's promise of the land to the Israelites, the Israelite scribes clarified the status of the Ishmaelites. In biblical times, the Ishmaelites were Arab people who lived around the Red Sea, and the stories about them probably were first told by word of mouth to explain their origins.[84] Even though God's promise was limited to Isaac and his descendants, the Ishmaelites were respected as another great nation. Divine protection extended to all of Abraham's children.

God's call to Abraham was the beginning of the biblical history of the Jewish people. Israel was considered the promised land because of the Lord's promise to give the land to Abraham's descendants through his son Isaac. The Romans named the area Palestine, destroyed its temple in the year 70 CE, and destroyed Jerusalem in the year 135 CE. Despite the dispersion of Jewish people to other regions, many looked forward to a messianic age when they would return to the Holy Land, and some see the establishment of the modern state of Israel as part of a gradual dawning of that age.[85]

Christianity shifted its focus from the promised land to the coming of God's kingdom and replaced circumcision with baptism to signify belonging to the Lord. As portrayed in the New Testament, Jesus, the son of God, was born into a Jewish family descending from Abraham, and God blesses all people through Abraham by their faith in his offspring Jesus. Abraham himself is considered a model of faith because he obeyed the call to the promised land and trusted the assurance of descendants as numerous as the stars.[86]

The Koran, the central religious text of Islam, says Abraham was "neither Jew nor Christian" but "an upright man, one who submitted to God."[87] Based on Islamic tradition interpreting the Koran, the Lord told Abraham to take Hagar and Ishmael to Mecca in what is now Saudi Arabia. Upon the Lord's instruction, Abraham and Ishmael restored the Kaaba, a sanctuary considered the house of God. Afterward the Lord told Abraham to call all the people of the world to make a pilgrimage there, and Abraham and Ishmael performed the rituals at the first pilgrimage. Muslims are still encouraged to go on this annual pilgrimage called the hajj at least once in their lifetime.[88]

In recent decades, more attention has been given to the stark reality of Hagar's situation. While still a teenager, she was a slave in a foreign country for an abusive mistress who ordered sexual relations with the master of the household. After Hagar fled, returning to the household may have been the only way for a pregnant woman to have survived. When Hagar and her son were cast out of the household into the wilderness, God as their only protector helped them survive a near-death experience and flourish in a new community. Calling Hagar's story a text of terror, my seminary professor Phyllis Trible concludes that "we who are heirs of Sarah and Abraham, by flesh and spirit, must answer for the terror"; and Delores Williams, another professor at my seminary, says the story shows how God helps African American women "make a way out of no way" by involvement in their struggle for survival and quality of life.[89]

Since the early days of Israel's history, Abraham's narrative has addressed our problems and given us hope for the future. People recall the touching encounters with the God of Old, they remember the promise of land and descendants, and they cherish Jewish, Christian, and Muslim traditions based on these stories. The God that hovered near Abraham, sometimes appearing as a person, assures all the patriarch's family a promising future.

LIVING BY THE STORY

Intrigued by Abraham's significance for Jews, Christians, and Muslims, my friends and I invited the imam of a Harlem mosque to discuss our common heritage. A towering African American man, he entered my apartment in an embroidered crown-shaped cap and long dark robe, accompanied by his bodyguard. After we sat down for dinner, the imam told us about his childhood. He was born into a Baptist family in the South during the segregated 1950s and raised as a Lutheran in New York City during the tumultuous 1960s. When he went off to college in the Lutheran heartland of my home state of Minnesota, instead of growing in Christian faith, he read *The Autobiography of Malcolm X*. After reading the book, the imam felt that Islam was closer to his social justice concerns and spiritual longings, and he decided to become a Muslim.

Once I heard about the personal experiences of the imam, I instantly felt a bond with him. Both of us knew what it was like to grow up in the Lutheran church, live in Minnesota, and attend college there; both of us had moved to New York City in search of a better life; and both of us looked for a faith that cared about the injustices of our past and not just a personal sense of spirituality.

Talking with the imam gave me a deeper understanding of the heritage Jews, Christians, and Muslims share as children of Abraham. God as portrayed in Abraham's story seems to be a spiritual presence hovering near us and watching out for us. If the going is rough, this presence may help us out of a rut and nudge us in a better direction. Just as God pointed Abraham to the stars, a spiritual presence may open our eyes to more possibilities than we had dared to dream. This may have been the flicker of hope that set me on the path that led to New York City. For each of us, Abraham's story may provide a way to envision a better life for ourselves.

6

Calling for Isaac's Sacrifice

How can we live by enduring values when cultural standards change over time?
GENESIS 22:1–19 (ABRAHAM'S NEAR SACRIFICE OF HIS SON)

EVER SINCE I FIRST read the Supreme Court's decision in Roe v. Wade, I realized how much the views we hold with moral or religious certainty about life and death may differ and shift over time. Some women I know believe that they should have the right to choose an abortion at any time up to a child's birth. But I know other women who consider abortion immoral. To them, it violates the sanctity of human life and is akin to killing a child. In the face of such divergent views, the Supreme Court asserted a constitutional right to abortion in Roe, which invalidated the laws of at least forty-nine and perhaps all the states. Nearly fifty years later, the Supreme Court overruled Roe, which again allowed legislatures to decide abortion laws.[90]

Like the abortion issue today, child sacrifice seemed to arouse passion and disagreement among the Israelites. In the early days of biblical Israel, the practice appeared to be accepted, at least under extraordinary circumstances. But attitudes toward child sacrifice changed dramatically in later years. The practice was considered more and more abhorrent and finally eradicated.

If we keep the historical context in mind, the Bible's story about Abraham nearly sacrificing his son Isaac is easier to understand. In the story, God tests Abraham's faith by seeing whether he would be willing to sacrifice his son when the Lord tells him to do so. If the Israelites considered child sacrifice akin to murder, God would have been ordering a heinous immoral act. Even though God ultimately prevented the sacrifice, the command still would have been troubling. If we believe that God sometimes commands us to do immoral acts and that we should do whatever God commands, any madman can claim God told him to kill someone.

If instead the Israelites considered child sacrifice a profound religious ritual, God would have been commanding an act of extreme devotion. From this perspective, Abraham was tested to see whether he would truly live by his commitment to the Lord. The story makes the dramatic point that even a parent's love for a child should be secondary to loving God and living God's way.

By looking at the historical setting, we can make sense of a story that otherwise seems incomprehensible to many modern readers. In its historical context, the story asked Abraham to perform an emotionally wrenching but not immoral act to show his commitment to the Lord. The story is a reminder to put God first because the Lord is bigger, better, and more valuable than anything else we hold dear. Within this context, God's test is a reminder to align our conduct and relationships with our deepest moral and spiritual values.

THE BIBLE'S STORY

Genesis 22 begins by saying that God was testing Abraham. Although the reader knows that God was simply setting up a test, Abraham did not know this. To modern readers, God would already have known how Abraham would respond because God is expected to know everything. But Israelites would not have made that assumption. They would have assumed God needed to test Abraham to find out whether he would obey divine commands under trying circumstances.[91]

When God called Abraham's name, he responded, "Here I am," and God told him to take "your son, your only son Isaac, whom you love," and offer him as a sacrifice.[92] Just as Abraham had left his family of origin for the land God would show him, he went to make the sacrifice on a mountain God would show him. The passage emphasized that this was his beloved son, the child of God's promise, and his hope for progeny. The placement of the passage after Ishmael's banishment intensified its emotional impact.

Abraham rose early in the morning, saddled his donkey, cut wood for the offering, took two young men and his son Isaac, and set out on the journey. He told the young men to wait with the donkey until he returned with his son from worship. After Abraham took the fire and a knife, and put wood for the offering on Isaac's back, the two of them walked onward together.

On the way, as told in Genesis 22:7, Isaac called his father's name, and his father responded, "Here I am, my son." Isaac observed that they had the fire and wood for the offering but asked about the lamb. In a response either poignant or perplexing, depending on your perspective, Abraham said that "God himself will provide the lamb."[93]

When they came to the place indicated by God, Abraham built an altar, bound Isaac, and laid him on top of the wood on the altar. Then Abraham reached out his hand and took the knife to kill his son.

At this moment, an angel called Abraham from heaven. As told in Genesis 22:11–12, after he again responded, "Here I am," the angel told him not to lay a hand on the boy or do anything to him, "for now I know that you fear God, since you have not withheld your son, your only son, from me."

When Abraham looked up, he saw a ram caught in a thicket by its horns, he made an offering of the ram instead of his son, and he named the place "The LORD will provide."[94] Then the angel called a second time in Genesis 22:16–18, telling him that the Lord says: "Because you have done this, and have not withheld your son, your only son, I will indeed bless you, and I will make your offspring as numerous as the stars . . . and by your offspring shall all the nations of the earth gain blessing for themselves."

Afterward Abraham returned to his young men and went home. Isaac's whereabouts at this point were not mentioned, his mother later died, and he never again appeared with his father in the Bible. Isaac found comfort in marrying Rebekah and raising a family with her.

In short, God tested whether Abraham would obey a divine command even if it meant giving up his precious son. With heart-wrenching resolve, Abraham proved his obedience by the near sacrifice of his son, and once Abraham passed the test, he was allowed to substitute a ram and was richly rewarded for his obedience. The emotional intensity of the account shows the difficulty of putting God first. But Abraham never wrestled with the morality of killing a child or questioned the divine claim on the child. Abraham assumed that the Lord could rightfully command the sacrifice of his son.

WRITING THE STORY

The historical context of the story indicates why Abraham never questioned God's command to sacrifice his son. Jon Levenson, a professor focusing on the Hebrew Bible at Harvard Divinity School, explains that the Israelites practiced child sacrifice early in their history, and even though the practice later ended, the idea of sacrificing a beloved son continued to influence Jewish and Christian rituals and narratives.[95] In accordance with this explanation, the story about Abraham's near sacrifice of his son may have originated when child sacrifice was still practiced, and the Israelites may have continued developing the story after child sacrifice was opposed and even eradicated.

The Bible itself indicates that child sacrifice was practiced in some circumstances. In 2 Kings 3:27, Israel was winning a battle against its enemy, but then the enemy's king sacrificed his firstborn son and afterward the Israelites were forced to retreat.

If we go back to the oldest legal material in the Bible's first five books, we find in Exodus 22:29–30 the claim that the firstborn son belongs to God. In the text God says: "The firstborn of your sons you shall give to me. You shall do the same with your oxen and with your sheep." The Lord's claim apparently was based on the deity's provision of life, land, and sustenance. Although the command was absolute, this did not mean it was routinely obeyed. Like many biblical laws, the command was never intended to be a rigidly enforced legal obligation. It expressed instead a religious ideal of devotion that could be observed in extraordinary circumstances.[96]

Eventually, laws now in Exodus 34:19–20 required the Israelites to redeem their firstborn sons from God's claim, perhaps by sacrificing a sheep. But the Israelites seemed to uphold child sacrifice as an ideal even if they could substitute an animal for the child. Like them, their Canaanite neighbors practiced child sacrifice and, at some point, could substitute a sheep or another animal for the child. But its substitution was not mandatory, and animal sacrifices did not entirely replace child sacrifice. The sacrifice of a child represented the most precious possible offering.[97]

In the late seventh and early sixth centuries BCE, the prophets Jeremiah and Ezekiel vehemently attacked child sacrifice. Jeremiah considered the practice so abhorrent to God that those engaging in it must be worshiping another deity. Taking a different tack, Ezekiel suggested that child sacrifice was a bad law God had designed to humiliate the Israelites and make them return to the Lord with greater devotion. Around the same time that these prophets opposed child sacrifice, legal codes now in Deuteronomy and Leviticus prohibited the practice. These prophets and legal codes did not require the substitution of an animal for a firstborn child. They did not recognize any claim whatsoever that God had on a child. The opposition to child sacrifice was so successful that the practice had completely stopped by the end of the sixth century BCE.[98]

When the Israelites scribes were writing their narrative during the Babylonian exile in the sixth century BCE, they incorporated the ancient narrative about Abraham and his son even though child sacrifice was waning and condemned. We do not know how much the exiles reshaped the story. But we do know that the story depicts a dire threat to Abraham's future like the threat to the exiles of Babylonian domination. The story may have encouraged the exiles to follow the Lord's command and trust the Lord's provision for their welfare no matter how difficult it may have been for the exiles to believe in the divine promise of a better future.[99]

According to some scholars, the story of Isaac's near death was intended to end child sacrifice among the Israelites or at least explain why they no longer sacrificed their children. Unlike other gods, Israel's God did not require Abraham to kill his child. But other scholars dispute this view. If the story was intended to end child sacrifice, why did the angel keep repeating how much Abraham would be blessed for his willingness to sacrifice his child? Abraham was assured a multitude of descendants precisely because he had been willing to sacrifice his son. According to these scholars, Abraham assumed that his child could be taken by the Lord, and he never considered child sacrifice the same as murder. The story emphasized his heartbreaking choice to put God first even if it meant the loss of his son.[100]

After the biblical text was finalized, the understanding of the story in Jewish, Muslim, and Christian faith continued to evolve. In Jewish synagogues, the text is called "The Akedah" or "Binding of Isaac" and read on the second day of Rosh Hashanah, the Jewish New Year. The rabbis traditionally praised Abraham for his faithful obedience to God's command, and sometimes held up Isaac as a martyr willing to participate in his own sacrifice. After the Holocaust, some Jewish writers were reluctant to endorse violence in religion's name and contended Abraham should have protested Isaac's sacrifice the way that Abraham questioned God's destruction of the cities of Sodom and Gomorrah.[101]

CALLING FOR ISAAC'S SACRIFICE

In Christian churches, the biblical text about Abraham's near sacrifice is sometimes called "The Sacrifice of Isaac." Similar to Abraham giving up Isaac, the New Testament proclaims that "God so loved the world that he gave his only Son" so that everyone believing in him would have eternal life.[102] As described in the New Testament, by faith, Abraham when tested offered up Isaac, considering "that God is able even to raise someone from the dead."[103] As this passage has been interpreted, God has sovereign freedom to demand the killing of a child. But God tempers this freedom with providential concern for our welfare as shown by the substitution of the ram.[104]

In Muslim tradition, Abraham's near sacrifice of his son is remembered by sacrificing a ram during the annual pilgrimage to Mecca. According to the Koran, Abraham dreamed that he was sacrificing his son and told his son about the dream. The son responded, "Father, do as you are bidden. God willing, you shall find me steadfast"; and after Abraham laid his son down upon his face, God called out, saying, "Abraham, you have fulfilled your vision."[105] But the Koran does not clarify whether the son was Isaac or Ishmael. Although some Islamic scholars named Isaac and placed the sacrifice in Jerusalem, others named Ishmael and placed the sacrifice in Mecca.[106]

As suggested by Levenson, if we consider the historical context of child sacrifice, we may change our interpretation of Abraham's near sacrifice of his son. Even though we no longer find child sacrifice acceptable, we can understand the difficulty of making the right choice when our personal inclinations conflict with our moral and spiritual values. We still need courage to live the way our deepest moral and spiritual values compel us to live. When we waiver in our resolve to do the right thing, we can find inspiration in Abraham's courage.

LIVING BY THE STORY

Whenever my friends and I discussed Abraham's near sacrifice of his son, the story evoked strong reactions. Several people were so horrified by such a grisly act that they refused to even consider child sacrifice in its historical context. As Emma explained, while she was growing up in a Catholic family, when she pictured a knife at Isaac's throat, "That was enough to be turned off religion for good." Josh, a strong supporter of Jewish causes, dismissed the idea that the story assumes God could claim a firstborn son. Josh said,

"That's not what the rabbis say. They say the story makes it clear that child sacrifice is wrong. God stopped Abraham before he killed his son." Elizabeth, a staunch Catholic, saw the story as a foretelling of God's sacrifice of his son for our salvation. She said, "To show the depth of God's love for us, God the father was willing to sacrifice his son Jesus, just as Abraham showed his love for God by his willingness to sacrifice his son Isaac."

Although I can understand these reactions, I do not see the story that way. To me, it is an austere, powerful story about commitment to our deepest values. The key to this understanding is the distinction between the morality of killing a child and the emotional difficulty of putting God first. By the standards of ancient culture, God never asked Abraham to do anything immoral because child sacrifice was not considered wrong. Rather, God asked him to show his commitment to the Lord even if it was emotionally excruciating, and in response, Abraham made the courageous choice to put God first.

Given that the Bible was written in different times and places over the course of a thousand years and that it was completed about two thousand years ago, we should not be surprised that it reflects diverse moral standards and sometimes varies from our standards today. The Bible itself shows us how to assess the evolving views on child sacrifice. At first, the oldest passages reflected the attitude toward child sacrifice in the local culture. Later, the prophets Jeremiah and Ezekiel vehemently disapproved of the practice because it was contrary to their understanding of God. Perhaps God leads us to different moral standards at different times, or perhaps we misunderstand God's direction at one time and gain more clarity at another time. That is why we need to keep evaluating the best way to resolve difficult moral questions such as the abortion controversy in our era.

I revisited the story of Abraham's near sacrifice of his son when a friend invited me to The 92nd Street Y in New York City for a lecture by Elie Wiesel. As a Holocaust survivor, Wiesel brought a distinctive perspective to the story. He talked about his own love for Isaac, the anguish Isaac must have felt, and the pain that would always remain with him. Yet Isaac survived the ordeal, got married, had children, seemed to enjoy life, and is still remembered today. Wiesel called Isaac the first survivor in Jewish history and a model for later survivors.[107]

From this perspective, Wiesel recognized a path to a good life despite the pain of the past. After listening to his lecture, I still admired Abraham's courage to live by his deepest values, but I also admired Isaac's resilience

Calling for Isaac's Sacrifice

in surviving a horrific ordeal. While Abraham symbolizes devotion to our highest ideals, Isaac portrays a survivor's strength. Today we need to keep reevaluating cultural practices based on our ultimate values just as Jeremiah and Ezekiel reevaluated child sacrifice based on their understanding of God. But we still need Abraham's courage to live by our highest values and Isaac's resilience to overcome adversity.

7

Jacob Wrestling with God

When your conduct goes awry, how do you take stock of your life and find a better path?

GENESIS 28:10–19 (JACOB'S LADDER TO HEAVEN);
32:24–31(JACOB WRESTLING WITH GOD);
33:1–11 (JACOB RECONCILING WITH BROTHER)

SOME YEARS AGO I attended a church conference on religion in the workplace. One of the participants was a recently retired businessman who had risen through the ranks to head his company. I asked him if he ever felt that he had compromised his values to get ahead. He said he had started out in a division of the company where he was judged by the division's profits and losses. As long as he stayed in that division, he felt the measure of his success was clear-cut. But after a few years he aspired to rise higher in the firm. To do so, he realized that he needed to be better known throughout his company as well as by the public. So he developed a plan to publicize his accomplishments in his company and elsewhere. Although he said he never lied, he admitted that "perhaps sometimes I took more credit for myself and gave less to others than the situation warranted."

His assessment rang true to me. In large law firms, though ambitious, most lawyers I knew wanted to maintain their reputation for high-quality work, and enough people were involved in their practice that someone was likely to catch and rectify any lapses. Still, among my acquaintances, several lawyers were dismissed for practicing law without a license or went to prison for tax fraud or insider trading, and outside of the office, a sibling colluded with a parent to get most of the inheritance, and spouses walked off with new lovers and much of the money from their marriages. More tragic, a friend of mine had a relative who killed his wife, and another acquaintance had a relative who killed his brother. The crimes were so unspeakable that the families broke apart in disbelief and grief.

Despite my observations of ambition, greed, and rage in businesses and families, I was shocked by the biblical stories about Isaac's son Jacob. Jacob was a shrewd man who used unscrupulous tactics to get ahead. He deceived his father, defrauded his brother, outwitted his father-in-law, and wrestled with God. Yet he found divine favor. God passed down the promise of land, descendants, and blessings from Abraham to Isaac to Jacob, and each of Jacob's twelve sons became the father of one of the twelve tribes of Israel. In my own life, the financial shenanigans of my mother and stepfather had caused me so much trouble and pain that biblical characters with similar flaws were deeply troubling. I did not think fraud should be rewarded, especially by God.

I developed greater appreciation for Jacob after studying the Bible's origins. Stories about him can be traced back to village life early in Israel's history. At that time, cunning and drive such as Jacob displayed would have helped villagers survive and thrive amid their powerful neighbors. Instead of expecting biblical characters to exemplify morality, I now see them as people like us, learning to live in an imperfect world, sometimes reconciling with and other times recoiling from a spiritual force bringing order to our lives.

THE BIBLE'S STORY

In Jacob's story in Genesis 25:19—37:1, we know from the beginning that Jacob is destined for a great future. Isaac and his wife Rebekah had twin sons, Esau and Jacob. While Isaac loved Esau, Rebekah loved Jacob. When the twins struggled with each other during her pregnancy, God told Rebekah that two nations were in her womb, one would be stronger than the other, and the elder would serve the younger. At birth, Esau came out first, hairy and red, the words for which in Hebrew suggested the nation of Edom. Then his brother came out gripping Esau's heel and was called Jacob, which meant "he takes by the heel" or "he supplants."[108] Even though Esau was born first, Jacob would supplant him as the forebear of Israel, resigning Esau to the less regarded nation of Edom.

As told in Genesis 25:29–34, taking Esau's birthright was Jacob's first step to supplant his brother. Because Esau was the oldest son, his birthright normally would have given him leadership of the family and a double portion of the inheritance. When Esau came home famished after a day of hunting, Jacob refused to give his brother anything to eat unless he sold his birthright. Considering it useless if he died of hunger, Esau sold it. The story never disapproved of Jacob for taking advantage of a hungry or shortsighted brother. It simply concluded, "Thus Esau despised his birthright."[109]

As told in Genesis 27:1–38, Jacob supplanted Esau again by taking away Isaac's deathbed blessing of his firstborn. To ancient people, deathbed blessings shaped the character and destiny of those blessed, and Isaac's blessing would have been especially powerful since it transferred the divine promise of land, descendants, and blessings given to Abraham and Isaac. Isaac was getting old, his eyesight was failing, and he did not know how much longer he would live. He asked Esau to hunt game to eat before giving him his blessing. When Rebekah overheard Isaac's request, she told Jacob to impersonate Esau so that Isaac would bless Jacob instead of Esau. Then she prepared food from the flock and dressed Jacob in Esau's clothes. Although Isaac was suspicious of Jacob's identity, he blessed him anyway. Just then, Esau returned from hunting and brought his father food. When Isaac realized that he had been deceived, he trembled violently, and Esau responded with a bitter cry. But in the view of ancient Israelites, the blessing could not be retracted.[110]

After Rebekah learned that Esau was planning to kill Jacob, she sent Jacob off to her brother Laban. When Jacob stopped at a place called Bethel, as described in Genesis 28:10–19, he dreamed of a ladder or staircase reaching from the earth to heaven, with angels going up and down. In this dream, the Lord said that he was the God of Abraham and Isaac, he would give the land to Jacob and his offspring, and all the families of the earth would be blessed in them. Through the dream, Jacob found out that he was favored by God soon after he had usurped his brother's blessing.

Although Jacob quickly fell in love with Laban's younger daughter, Rachel, Jacob worked for Laban for seven years before he would permit marriage. After seven years, Laban made a marriage feast, but substituted his older daughter, Leah, for Rachel on the wedding night. When Jacob woke up the next morning, he was shocked to see Leah lying beside him.

In stark contrast to Jacob taking the blessing intended for his elder brother, Laban explained that the younger does not marry before the elder and required Jacob to work another seven years to marry Rachel. Jacob eventually had twelve sons and a daughter with his wives, Leah and Rachel, and his two concubines. While he stayed with Laban, Jacob also became prosperous, outwitting his father-in-law in a deal for ownership of the flocks. After twenty years, Jacob returned home with his large family and many possessions.

In Genesis 32, while Jacob was traveling home, he feared Esau's desire for revenge, asked for God's protection, and sent gifts ahead to his brother. The night before the brothers met, Jacob moved all his family and possessions across a stream. Left alone on the other side, he unknowingly fought a man who turned out to be God. Jacob was so strong that he was winning the fight. After the man saw that he was losing, he struck Jacob in the hip socket and pulled his hip out of joint.

At daybreak, the man wanted to leave, but Jacob would not release him without a blessing. When the man asked his name, he replied, "Jacob," with all its connotations of supplanting. The man told him that he would no longer be called Jacob, but Israel, for "you have striven with God and with humans and have prevailed."[111] The name apparently referred to successfully striving with Esau, Isaac, Laban, and now God. After receiving the blessing, Jacob renamed the place Penuel, meaning "the face of God," explaining, "For I have seen God face to face, yet my life is preserved."[112] As the sun rose, he left Penuel, limping because of the blow to his hip.

In Genesis 33, when Jacob looked up, he saw Esau coming with four hundred men. As Jacob prepared for the worst, Esau ran to meet, embrace, and kiss him, and both men wept. Esau initially rejected any gifts by saying, "I have enough, my brother; keep what you have for yourself," but later accepted the gifts in response to Jacob's urging, "No, please; if I find favor with you, then accept my present from my hand, for truly to see your face is like seeing the face of God."[113] Afterward Esau suggested they stay together. Ever the deceiver, Jacob sent his brother ahead, promised to follow, and then went elsewhere. The brothers met again to bury their father, Isaac.

WRITING THE STORY

Like the exodus story, stories about Jacob were passed along by word of mouth during Israel's tribal period before it had a king. At that time, the

Israelites had a precarious existence, and like other vulnerable communities, they celebrated tricksters who survived against the odds by deceiving and defeating more powerful opponents. As the Israelites became a more established society, they wrote down and updated the stories to reflect contemporary concerns.

Back in the tribal period, the Israelites were dependent on many circumstances beyond their control. They lived on a subsistence level in small hilltop villages in the central highlands, growing crops and raising a few animals. Families would store food from their harvests and water from the rainy season. But every three or four years, the rain would be too little to grow sufficient crops. During such times, households struggled to survive until the next rainy season resulted in better crops. Besides unstable food and water supplies, the villagers had little protection against raids from nearby neighbors or foreign invaders because the villagers lacked the walled cities and standing armies of the city-state kingdoms and large empires of the ancient Near East. Men who survived early childhood typically lived into their mid-thirties. Women often died by their late twenties, half in childbirth.[114]

Given the hazards of tribal life, the Israelite villagers admired a trickster like Jacob who could survive by his wits and win against the odds. He was an underdog who succeeded by cunning, tricks, and lies. If we are part of a dominant culture, we are likely to value playing by the rules and disapprove of people who break them. To downtrodden people, the rules may seem stacked against them, and underhanded tactics may seem the only way to beat the system. When the Israelites heard stories about Jacob, his cunning and drive inspired them to prevail despite their harsh circumstances. Eventually all the Israelites regarded Jacob as their common ancestor, uniting them in their struggle to survive.[115]

During the monarchy of David and Solomon, their scribes were more interested in the literary traditions of ancient Near Eastern empires than the stories passed down by the Israelite tribes. The stories about Jacob acquired greater significance after Solomon died, when the monarchy divided into a Southern Kingdom ruled from Jerusalem and a Northern Kingdom north of the city. To distinguish itself from the Davidic monarchy, the Northern Kingdom developed its own literature to legitimize its rule. In doing so, its scribes wrote down and compiled stories about Jacob, and they used the stories to enhance the northern royal sanctuary city of Bethel, where Jacob saw a staircase to heaven, and the early northern capital city of Penuel, where Jacob wrestled with God.[116]

During the Babylonian exile, the Israelites apparently added to Jacob's story the promise of land, descendants, and blessings from Abraham through Isaac to Jacob. In the earliest version of his journey at Bethel, Jacob may have dreamed of a stairway with divine messengers going up and down between heaven and earth. In a later version, the Lord appeared in the dream to assure Jacob that he would benefit from the promise. By this addition, the wily ancestor who had inspired Israelite tribes early in their history was linked to Abraham in a narrative that gave hope to exiles living in despair.[117]

Accepting the rough aspects of Jacob's character is sometimes challenging for people of faith today. The views of Pope Benedict XVI, serving from 2005 to 2013, are notable in this regard because Pope Benedict was a biblical scholar. He acknowledged that the Bible includes dark passages that feature immoral acts of cheating and trickery, and he emphasized that human nature has always had a dark side. He also asked us to look at the biblical stories in the context of the culture and morality of their time.[118]

Pope Benedict still found the biblical stories emblematic of our life with God. The pope said that Jacob's wrestling match "speaks to us about a long night of seeking God." When God asked Jacob his name, it revealed "his true identity as a deceiver, one who supplants," and when Jacob recognized he was battling with God, he was given "a new name as a sign of a new identity." Contrary to Jacob's initial demand, a blessing from God cannot be taken or won by force, but must be received with humility, as "a gratuitous gift that ultimately allows us to recognize the Lord's face."[119]

The pope's description helps to bridge the gap between Jacob as a trickster and Jacob as an esteemed Israelite patriarch. The scribes compiling his narrative placed his wrestling match with the divine at a pivotal point in his life. The match honors his ambition and success while suggesting a more troubling aspect of his life. After wrestling with God, he leaves with a limp but also a new identity truer to himself.

LIVING BY THE STORY

Early in Israel's history, the trickster tradition helps us appreciate Jacob as an underdog striving to get ahead. Even if he cut a few corners, his wrestling match with God suggests divine acceptance and a path forward.

When choosing an heir to Abraham's promise, the Lord was not constrained by the undesirable conduct in Jacob's past or social conventions about a firstborn's rights. We can be a force for good despite our past misdeeds and society's expectations. Even so, the wrestling match reminds us of those times when our lives are out of kilter and need to be brought in line with our deepest values.

In practicing criminal law, my colleague George has a great deal of experience with out-of-kilter lives. He defends people charged with white-collar crimes, violent conduct, and scuffles with the police. In his line of work, he is well acquainted with immoral, unethical, and unjust departures from ordinary social standards. He counsels clients that criminal behavior is always entwined with our personal lives. He says, "People don't just break the law in an isolated incident. Something in their personal lives isn't working." He encourages his clients to repair whatever needs to be fixed and build a better life for themselves.

Jacob's foibles seem to be an acknowledgment that God does not demand perfection. We can use our talents despite our flaws to benefit our families and communities. But if our striving at home or work becomes excessive, we may find ourselves struggling with a subliminal power to bring our actions back in line. Though blessed with divine favor, even Jacob had to face up to his past, struggle with God, and leave with a limp. Wrestling with God can be a metaphor for taking stock of where we have been, where we are going, and how to find a better path.

8

Divine Providence in Joseph's Life

Have you ever sensed a spiritual force moving toward a positive outcome despite people intending harm?

GENESIS 45:4–8 (GOD'S PROVIDENCE); 50:15–21 (GOD USING FOR GOOD WHAT IS MEANT FOR HARM)

WHENEVER I VISITED MY family's farm with my New York friends, the dogs would bark as soon as our car turned toward the farmhouse. Eager to welcome us, Grandpa and Uncle Bill would come out of the barn or drive up on a tractor, Grandma would emerge from the henhouse with a basket of eggs, and Aunt Mary would wave from the garden. The warmth of our reception was set against a backdrop of peeling paint on broken-down buildings. Struck by the contrast between my rural roots and my career as a New York lawyer, my friends would say how touching it was to watch my relatives come over to greet and hug me. As one friend put it, "They welcomed you with open arms."

When I contrasted this bucolic picture with the destructive tendency of my mother and stepfather, I took comfort in the Bible's story about Jacob's son Joseph. Despite the treachery of his brothers, Joseph rose to the top of the Egyptian government and saved the world from famine. Throughout these events, he never had the direct encounters with God that characterized the relationship of Abraham and Jacob with the divine. Instead, Joseph grew to understand that God was shaping events while staying behind the scenes. As Joseph expressed the story's maxim, what others intend for harm, God can still use for good.

My life seemed to reflect this maxim. My mother and stepfather's attempts to block my education and career were ultimately stymied. Instead of thwarting me, they made me more determined to create a better life for myself. Although I never had direct encounters with God, I felt in later years as if a spiritual force had provided for me through the events in my life.

By studying the origins of Joseph's story, we can deepen our understanding of its maxim. Like people in our modern secular culture, the sages of the ancient wisdom tradition developed a restrained view of divine intervention in the world. As Joseph's story interpreted these tenets, we are free to choose our actions, and we are responsible for our conduct. Nevertheless, regardless of our good or bad intentions, we cannot ultimately frustrate the divine plan, and our actions can be used to fulfill its purposes. Joseph's story affirms our freedom to act in the present while remaining optimistic about the future by trusting in a providential force moving toward a beneficial outcome.

THE BIBLE'S STORY

Joseph's story is considered a narrative masterpiece. The elaborate account is told in chapters 37–50 at the end of Genesis.

As the story begins in Genesis 37:1, Jacob has fathered twelve sons with Leah and Rachel and their maids. He favored Rachel's elder son, Joseph, and next in line was her younger son, Benjamin. Jacob made his favoritism clear by giving an ornate robe to Joseph, who in turn stoked his siblings' jealousy by tattling on them and telling them about his dreams. The dreams suggested that one day the entire family would bow down to him.

As the story continues in Genesis 37:12, enraged by envy, Joseph's brothers decided to kill him while they were grazing their father's flocks. When a caravan of merchants passed by on their way to Egypt, a brother named Judah proposed selling Joseph to the traders instead of murdering him. Afterward the brothers dipped his robe in goat's blood so that their father would assume Joseph had been killed by a ferocious animal.

In Genesis 39–40, the caravan proceeded to Egypt, where Joseph was sold to Potiphar, the captain of the pharaoh's guard. Because the Lord was with Joseph, he was put in charge of everything Potiphar owned; and after Potiphar's wife made false accusations, landing Joseph in prison, Joseph was put in charge of all the inmates. When the pharaoh's chief cupbearer and baker were sent to prison, Joseph interpreted their dreams with God's help to mean the cupbearer would be restored to his position and the baker would be executed. Shortly thereafter things turned out exactly as Joseph said.

In Genesis 41, two years later when the pharaoh was confused by his dreams, the cupbearer referred him to Joseph. In the dreams, Joseph said God was revealing that seven years of abundance would be followed by seven years of famine. He advised the pharaoh to put a wise and discerning man in charge of the land so that grain could be stored during the abundant years and used for food during the famine. Because God had shown all this to Joseph, the pharaoh concluded that no one was wiser or more discerning. He put Joseph in charge of the entire land, and after the famine began, the whole world came to him to buy grain.

In Genesis 42, since Jacob's family was suffering from the worldwide famine, Jacob instructed his sons to buy grain in Egypt. But he did not send Joseph's brother, Benjamin, for fear he might be harmed. When the ten brothers met Joseph, they did not recognize him and unknowingly bowed down before him, just as he once had dreamed. After hearing that Benjamin had stayed home, Joseph demanded that one brother be kept in prison until the others returned with Benjamin. Even though the brothers did not realize Joseph's identity, they considered his demand divine punishment and recalled Joseph's distress when pleading for his life. Then one brother stayed in prison while the others went back to get Benjamin. But Jacob would not let Benjamin go to Egypt. He callously told his sons that with Joseph dead, Benjamin was the only one left.

In Genesis 43–44, after his family ran out of food, Jacob relented and sent Benjamin along with his other sons back to Egypt. Although Joseph privately wept over the sight of Benjamin, he still did not reveal his identity and instead planted a trap, perhaps to test his brothers or to keep Benjamin with him. He told his servant to hide Joseph's silver cup in Benjamin's sack and then accuse him of theft. When the brothers were brought back to Joseph, he agreed to take Benjamin as his slave and let the others leave. In a poignant moment, Judah empathized with Jacob's love for Benjamin, pleaded to let him return to his grieving father, and offered to remain instead as Joseph's slave. Judah's offer unknowingly redressed the suggestion he had made years ago to sell Joseph to the traders in the caravan going to Egypt.

Deeply moved, in Genesis 45:3–5, Joseph loudly wept and declared to his brothers: "I am Joseph. Is my father still alive?" In response to his brothers' terror upon learning his identity, he urged them not be distressed or angry at themselves for selling him into Egypt because "God sent me before you to preserve life." Joseph explained that God had sent him ahead of his brothers to save many lives during the famine. He asked them to tell Jacob how God had made Joseph the lord of all of Egypt, and to bring back Jacob to live there. Jacob was stunned to hear the news of his son, had a tearful reunion with him, and remained the rest of his life with his whole family in Egypt.

After Jacob died, Joseph's brothers were again afraid that he would take revenge for the wrongs they had done to him. In Genesis 50:19–20, Joseph reassured his brothers that they need not be afraid: "Am I in the place of God? Even though you intended to do harm to me, God intended it for good, in order to preserve a numerous people, as he is doing today." Joseph's statement is often considered the crux of the story and an insight into divine providence.

Joseph's story forms a crucial link to other events in the Bible. A subsequent pharaoh enslaved Jacob's descendants, who escaped from bondage during the exodus and then conquered the promised land. When David and Solomon formed a monarchy ruled from Jerusalem, they traced their lineage to Judah. After the monarchy divided into the Southern Kingdom in Jerusalem and the Northern Kingdom north of the city, the first king of the Northern Kingdom traced his lineage to Joseph. Following the destruction of the Northern Kingdom, Judah remained the forebear of Jerusalem's kings.

WRITING THE STORY

Joseph's story is a literary masterpiece, reflecting a royal, urban, and international culture. It appears to date back to the monarchical period, which came after tribal villagers told stories about Jacob and before the Babylonian exiles shaped Abraham's story. As a likely scenario, Joseph's narrative may have been written in the Northern Kingdom to bolster its first king, who traced his ancestry to Joseph, and Judah's role may have reflected the significance of Jerusalem in Israel's history.[120]

When the Israelites wrote Joseph's narrative, they probably took an earlier story written in Canaan or Egypt and adapted it to explain why

Jacob's family stayed in Egypt. In describing Joseph's descent into slavery and rise to the top of Egyptian society, the Israelite writers could have relied on distant memories of historical reality. People from Canaan frequently went to Egypt in times of famine because its irrigation system provided more reliable food supplies. Long ago, foreigners also had taken control of Egypt for a century or so before they were expelled.[121]

The original story underlying Joseph's narrative exemplified the values of the wisdom tradition in the ancient Near East. The sages who pursued wisdom often advised kings and interpreted dreams and other signs. They provided practical wisdom expressed in maxims for correct living and speculative wisdom regarding philosophical and religious issues. From the perspective of these sages, a divine plan underlies reality, everything happens according to this plan, wisdom helps us understand the principles underlying the plan, and patience is required while the plan unfolds. Typical of this tradition, Joseph was considered wise, advised a king, and interpreted dreams. He also exemplified patience while facing trying circumstances. He had the wisdom to know that everything would work out and the patience to wait for things to be resolved.[122]

In keeping with the wisdom tradition, Joseph's relationship to God was very different from the encounters of Abraham, Isaac, Jacob, and Hagar with the God of Old. These encounters featured visions of and interactions with the Lord and obedience to divine commands. Joseph never experienced such visions, interactions, or commands. He never even prayed to the Lord or thanked him for his deeds. God stayed behind the scenes, shaping events, and as Joseph matured, he became increasingly aware of divine involvement in these events.[123]

Walter Brueggemann, a contemporary American biblical scholar, analyzes why Joseph's story would appeal to a sophisticated, cosmopolitan audience.[124] In his view, the story was intended for people who were embarrassed by blatant expressions of faith and drawn to a more humanist view. They would be skeptical about God talking to Abraham or wrestling with Jacob; they would not identify with Abraham's willingness to leave his home and country or sacrifice his son on God's command; and they would question how much God intervenes to rescue them from their problems. Yet the author of Joseph's story wanted to show that God's purposes prevail beyond human limitations.

To solve this dilemma, Joseph's narrative illustrates how God shapes the scene without being in the scene. On one level, each person was free to make his own decisions and remained responsible for their consequences. On another level, an overarching spiritual presence helped to stave off famine, overcame acts done out of malice, and brought about the reconciliation of Joseph's family. As a bridge between these levels, Joseph recognized and cooperated with a divine hand at work in family dynamics and world affairs.

Brueggemann's analysis provides a broader perspective for Joseph's maxim that God can use for good what others intend for harm. Like the ancient sages, we can imagine a divine force underlying reality. Each of us can do our best to align our conduct with this force. Yet God's purposes do not depend on our actions. We can remain confident that the divine plan will prevail despite our own limitations and the shortcomings of others.

LIVING BY THE STORY

Joseph's story was well liked by my friends, who fit the description of the cosmopolitan audience anticipated by the people writing and adapting the story. In line with Brueggemann's assessment, these friends found it difficult to identify with blatant expressions of faith and were skeptical of supernatural events beyond scientific explanations. They liked the way the story affirms our freedom to act and conveys divine intervention as a subtle, hidden force. Portrayed this way, divine intervention seems less jarring to our sense of reality even if it is the force shaping our reality.

My friend Sophia declared Joseph her favorite character in the Bible. She appreciated the way he persevered and prevailed no matter what happened. As she said, "He always comes out on top." Given her upbringing in a working-class family, she was proud that she had made it through medical school, and admired people like herself who "pulled themselves up by their bootstraps." She praised Joseph's story for encouraging people to overcome obstacles and create a better life for themselves.

For my friend Hannah, the heart of the story was the reconciliation of Joseph's family, not his rise to the top. In the aftermath of her affair with a married man, she regretted the choices she had made, stopped drinking alcohol, and tried to compensate for any harm she inflicted on others. To help her in these efforts, she looked for friendships with spiritually inclined people. She liked Joseph's story because it illustrates how tapping into a spiritual presence improves our lives. To grow spiritually, she advocated practices demonstrated by Joseph and his brothers—admitting fault, making amends for wrongdoing, and forgiving others for hateful acts.

What I find most uplifting about Joseph's story is its portrayal of divine providence. At first, I was drawn to the story for its maxim that we can prevail despite other people undermining us. Now I see the implications of the maxim for our own conduct as well as others. We can take comfort that divine providence works around the shortcomings all of us have. Some people may question a divine role in this process. But even people who are not religious often remain optimistic about the future through belief in the evolution of humanistic values, or an underlying force for goodness, or a simple notion that things will eventually work out for the better.

Divine providence can help us remain optimistic when solving problems in our personal lives, our communities, and the world. Instead of feeling overwhelmed by the magnitude of our problems, trust in providential care keeps us from losing hope, no matter how difficult things may seem at the present time and no matter how long it takes to overcome these difficulties. Like Joseph and other ancient sages, we can seek wisdom to know things will work out and patience to wait for things to be resolved.

PART III

Finding Redemption

(Exodus)

9

Overcoming Adversity

How have you overcome adverse circumstances in your life?
EXODUS 1:8–22 (OPPRESSION OF ISRAELITES);
3:1–15 (MOSES AT BURNING BUSH)

AFTER THANKSGIVING DINNER, GRANDMA, then in her early seventies, asked me to pick one of her things as a keepsake. I knew immediately I wanted the picture that hung above my bed in the farmhouse. It showed a run-down bridge over a raging river during a fierce storm. On one side, an angel watched over a small girl making her way across the broken planks of the bridge. Under divine care, the girl headed toward a tranquil homestead in the horizon on the other side. To me, the angel was my grandmother saving me from my mother and stepfather by providing a safe haven on the farm.

When I consider my life story, I feel as though a divine presence rescued me from the detrimental consequences of parental abuse through my grandparents' love. Social scientists confirm the significance of my grandparents' role. Decades of research have considered why some children overcome significant adversity and others do not. The studies have covered numerous hardships, including poverty, neglect, violence, and parental mental illness and substance abuse. Regardless of the hardship, the single most common finding is that children who end up doing well have had at least one stable and committed relationship with a supportive parent, caregiver, or other adult. That adult buffers them from more severe disruptions and helps them build the skills to respond to adversity and thrive.[125]

No matter how big I dreamed, I could count on my grandmother's encouragement. In third grade, I wanted to be the first woman president of the United States. I was too embarrassed to tell anyone because the other girls in my class wanted to be nurses, teachers, and homemakers, and the boys wanted to be police officers and firefighters. One afternoon I found my grandmother alone in the farmhouse, kneading dough to bake the week's bread. I blurted out, "Grandma, what would you think if I became the president of the United States?" Without a moment's hesitation, she responded as if she had been expecting this question all along, "I would be like any grandmother. I would be so proud." From then on, I knew I could pursue whatever I wanted.

Because I found refuge on my grandparents' farm, I identify with the Israelites rescued from bondage by divine love. Their redemption dramatizes the fundamental idea that God saves people who are suffering or oppressed. In Hebrew Scripture, the Israelites repeatedly looked to God to deliver them from distress as God had done in the exodus, and to this day, the exodus story strengthens Jewish belief in redemption when facing oppression.[126] In a similar manner, Christians look to Jesus Christ as their redeemer to overcome sin and death and restore them to new life. Although Christians sometimes stress spiritual welfare, both the Old and New Testaments show divine concern with all aspects of our lives. The exodus story illustrates how much God cares about our physical, economic, and social well-being.[127]

God's deliverance of the Israelite slaves and Christ's life, death, and resurrection are the Bible's great stories of redemption. By looking to the past, both Jews and Christians live with hope for the future. They see how divine love has helped us in earlier times and will guide us through future difficulties. Redemption is such a pervasive concept in our culture that it shapes social movements and affects the way we tell our personal life stories even if we are not religious. By looking for ways that we have overcome past problems, we maintain hope that we will prevail in our current struggles.

THE BIBLE'S STORY

As reported at the beginning of the book of Exodus, the pharaoh was hospitable to Jacob and his family when they joined Joseph in Egypt. But after

Joseph died, his name meant nothing to the new pharaoh. Faced with the enormous growth of the Israelite population, the pharaoh feared that the Israelites would align themselves with Egypt's enemies, fight against the country, and escape from the land. To limit the population growth, taskmasters oppressed the Israelites with forced labor, building Pithom and Rameses for military purposes and working on other construction and agricultural projects. When forced labor was not enough to ease the pharaoh's concern about the growth of the Israelite population, the pharaoh commanded his people to throw every Israelite baby boy into the Nile.

As told in Exodus 2, after an Israelite mother gave birth to Moses, she placed him in a basket among the reeds along the bank of the Nile, while Moses's sister, Miriam, watched to see what would happen. When the pharaoh's daughter went down to the river to bathe, she discovered the Israelite baby and felt sorry for him. Miriam offered to find an Israelite woman to nurse him, and after the pharaoh's daughter agreed, Miriam returned him to his mother. When the baby was done nursing, his mother took him back to the pharaoh's daughter, who took him as her son.

Despite his royal upbringing, Moses identified with the Israelite people. When he saw an Egyptian beating an Israelite, he killed the Egyptian. As news of the murder spread, Moses feared for his life and fled the country. He married a woman whose father was a priest in the land of Midian in northwest Arabia. While Moses was tending his father-in-law's sheep, he came to "Horeb, the mountain of God," perhaps named as an indication of its sanctity for the Midianites.[128]

In Exodus 3, at Horeb, also called Sinai in the Bible, an angel of the Lord appeared to Moses in flames of fire within a bush. Moses saw that the bush did not burn up though it was on fire. When he went over to look at the strange sight, God called from within the bush: "Moses! Moses!" And he responded, "Here I am."[129] God told him to come no closer and take off his sandals for he was standing on holy ground.

Identifying himself as the God of Abraham, Isaac, and Jacob, the Lord said that he had seen the misery of the Israelites and would send Moses to the pharaoh to bring them out of Egypt to a fertile land flowing with "milk and honey," which is the Bible's first reference to Israel by this phrase.[130] When Moses questioned how he could do this, God said, "I will be with you."[131] Since people at that time believed in many gods and the generic term "god" could refer to any of them, Moses asked what to say if the Israelites wanted to know the name of their ancestors' god. The Lord responded,

"I AM WHO I AM," and told Moses to say "I AM" had sent him. As a third response, God said his name forever was "Yahweh."[132] Interestingly, all three of these puzzling names of the divine were based on a root not for a noun but for a verb meaning "to be." Another translation for the first response would be "I WILL BE WHAT I WILL BE," meaning "My nature will become evident from my actions."[133]

In a dramatic account of God's power, the rest of the story shows how Moses led the Israelites out of Egypt to Israel. They included six hundred thousand men on foot, together with women, children, and the elderly. Based on this description, the exodus saved more than two million people. The number probably was exaggerated to emphasize the fertility of the Israelites and the participation of all the Israelites in the exodus.[134]

WRITING THE STORY

The origins of the exodus story have been highly debated. No historical records or archaeological finds provide evidence for the movement of such a large group out of Egypt through the wilderness to Israel. Yet many biblical scholars believe an exodus of a smaller group did occur. When this group told their story, it was so inspiring that it was passed along by word of mouth from one generation to the next. At some point, the story was written down so that the entire community could keep reliving the experience.[135]

Egypt would be a realistic setting for the exodus story. Foreigners from western Asia periodically migrated to Egypt, especially during famines. Others were forced to go there as military captives of the Egyptians or human tribute sent by Canaanite rulers. Even if foreigners came voluntarily, they were often required to work on government projects. While most foreigners were integrated into Egyptian society, in at least one known instance, several workers escaped into the Sinai wilderness.[136]

Details of the exodus story and sources outside the Bible add credence to the exodus account. Even though the Bible says Moses's mother gave him his name because she drew him out of the water, Moses was actually an Egyptian name that meant "is born."[137] Both of the cities Pithom and Rameses have been associated with Egyptian locations, and Rameses was expanded by Pharaoh Rameses II, who reigned from 1279 to 1213 BCE. During the subsequent reign of Pharaoh Merneptah from 1213 to 1203 BCE, a granite slab extolled his military victory over a group identified as "Israel" in Canaan. This inscription is the first mention of Israel outside of the Bible. It coincides with archaeological evidence that indicates the Israelites were living in Canaan around the same time. For such reasons, the exodus is often linked to the reign of Rameses II or Merneptah.

The venerable history of the exodus story and its significance to Israelite tradition also suggest that it really happened. Some of the oldest passages in the Bible recount the story, and key Israelite traditions such as Passover have celebrated the occasion since early times. In addition, the humble position of the Israelites in the story supports its credibility. While many national myths stress noble origins, the exodus was about slaves who escaped to another land with God's help. Such a story seems unlikely to have been invented by people to describe themselves unless it was based on some set of facts.

Considered from a historical perspective, the exodus probably involved a small group of people who had been living in Egypt and escaped from forced labor. When that group settled in the hill country of what became northern Israel, they praised God for rescuing them from slavery and told the people living in their new community about the Lord's intervention on their behalf. The local Canaanite residents were inspired by the story because they too had suffered from domination by Egyptian and other powerful groups. When these residents adopted the story as their own, it helped them fight their enemies and overcome adversity. Along with the descendants of ex-slaves, the Canaanite residents became the people known as the Israelites. Together, they worshiped Yahweh and shared the exodus story as their common heritage.

Eventually the exodus story was written down as the collective memory of the community. The key concern of the writers was not to record accurate details of the escape but rather to recreate the intense emotional experience of freedom from bondage. The significance of the event was further enhanced by incorporating agricultural festivals of the Israelites into the Passover celebration. By commemorating the past, the Israelites found inspiration to survive the Babylonian exile and other traumatic experiences.

Just as the exodus story inspired the Israelites in ancient times, it has continued to inspire people seeking freedom and justice throughout the centuries down to the present time. When the Puritans sailed for Massachusetts Bay in 1630, they believed their New World settlement would be like a new Israel. They felt that they had escaped their tormentors just as the Israelites had escaped the Egyptians and compared their leader John Winthrop to Moses.[138] More than two centuries later, some six hundred Black men, women, and children gathered in Washington, DC, the night before Abraham Lincoln issued the Emancipation Proclamation on January 1, 1863. When they sang "Go Down, Moses," they added another verse: "Go down, Abraham, away down in Dixie's land, tell Jeff Davis to let my people go."[139] For the escaped slaves, Lincoln was the new Moses and confederacy head Davis was the new pharaoh. To this day, the exodus continues to inspire oppressed people who fight for civil rights and social justice.

LIVING BY THE STORY

As part of the Judeo-Christian tradition, the exodus story has been so significant in our culture that it influences how we understand our personal experiences. From Hollywood movies to self-help books, we like to hear about people surmounting difficulties and making good on second chances. When we tell our life stories, we often describe redemptive experiences that change unfavorable conditions into a better future. That is the same way I tell my own story.

Dan McAdams, a psychology professor at Northwestern University, confirms that many Americans tell life stories with redemptive themes.[140] As a narrative psychologist, he studies personal stories we construct to give meaning, unity, and purpose to our lives. We talk about where we have been, where we are going, and what the turning points were. From time to time, we change our stories in light of new experiences or personal goals. Although the ways we construct our stories are not objectively verifiable, they form our identity, and they help us understand and cope with reality.

When Americans tell their life stories, McAdams finds a common theme of redemption, which he defines in the broad sense of deliverance from suffering to a better place. Even though the Judeo-Christian view of redemption has been influential in this country, he notes that the concept of redemption can be found in all the world's major religions and many cultural traditions and has both religious and secular meanings. The people he studies describe many kinds of redemption: they find freedom from oppression and abuse; they experience forgiveness for their sins; they struggle out of poverty to achieve educational, economic, and social standing; they overcome disabilities and mental and physical illness; they recover from alcoholism and addictions; they develop psychological maturity and moral character; and they gain insights into the person they feel they were meant to be.[141]

In McAdams's studies, the people who tell life stories with redemptive sequences moving from suffering to enhancement are more likely to enjoy better overall psychological well-being. They tend to have greater self-esteem and find their lives more meaningful and satisfying. Other studies help to explain why. After people suffer from a loss, illness, or other painful experience, talking about that experience often lessens pain and leads to better psychological and physical health. Many people see ways in which the suffering they experience leads to positive changes in their lives. And the people who see or imagine good things coming from bad events in their lives tend to cope better with those events and find ways to move forward in life.[142]

Besides improving personal well-being, redemptive life stories correlate with helping others have better lives. McAdams is intrigued by people who are highly involved in making the world a better place for future generations. They may do so by parenting, teaching, mentoring, volunteering, participating in religious, political, and civic organizations, or a variety of other activities. When such people talk to McAdams's research team, their life stories tend to have redemptive themes, and telling their stories this way may help them sustain their involvement with others. They often indicate that they were raised in religious homes, and early on, typically in adolescence, they developed beliefs and values rooted in religious tradition. Throughout the rest of their personal stories, these beliefs sustained their commitment to improving the world.[143]

Yet McAdams notes some problematic aspects of redemptive life stories. Some people focus too much on individual freedom instead of their families and communities, or they develop a sense of superiority that fails to take seriously other points of view, or they justify aggression or excessive moral fervor for misguided values, or they live with a naïve optimism that trivializes suffering or denies the tragedies of life. Considering these limitations, we may want to reexamine our life stories from time to time for ways they hinder our development.[144]

Like the people McAdams studies, my friend Emily considers redemption a key theme in her life. After she was diagnosed with polio at age five, her parents took her to one of the best medical centers for treatment. Two years later, a world-famous surgeon operated on her spine. Still, Emily struggled with the debilitating effects of polio throughout her childhood. In her twenties, she sought help from a therapist. Emily asked, "Why me?" And her therapist responded, "Why not you?" Emily explained, "I always wanted to know who I'd be if I hadn't had polio." To her surprise, the therapist said, "You're exactly the person you were meant to be." At that moment, Emily realized that she had a good life with good medical care, and she could help others overcome adversity. She said, "I feel my soul was put in the right body at the right time and place."

My friend Ben compares the Passover meal to Thanksgiving dinner commemorating the Pilgrims' harvest at Plymouth, Massachusetts. Just as Thanksgiving is a time for families to get together in their homes to celebrate an American tradition, Passover is a time for families to get together in their homes to affirm their Jewish identity. He feels that hearing the exodus story again and again makes Jews "hardwired for social justice." Another Jewish friend, Josh, calls the story "important to every Jew and to the world because it means we will always be free." When I questioned how this could be true, he answered, "That's why we say, 'Next year in Jerusalem,' at the end of every Passover. If not now, then. We keep hoping."

My most moving encounter with a Christian version of the exodus story occurred in a prison in Haiti. I went to the country with a church group to help my cousin Amy, who was there as a missionary after her husband Matt died of kidney failure. During our stay, we taught farmers better techniques for growing crops and visited people in their homes, school, hospital, and prison.

The prison was more squalid than I had imagined. Centered around a courtyard, it had three small, unfurnished, one-room buildings with prison bars on the side facing the courtyard and solid walls on the other sides. A tiny room housed a couple of young teens, including a boy who had murdered someone; another tiny room housed a few women; and a somewhat bigger room housed about a hundred men. During the day, the men stood shoulder to shoulder, crowded together in the dark space. At night, they took turns sleeping on the ground because the area was not big enough for everyone to lie down at the same time. Left without a toilet, they passed around a garbage bag for body waste.

My cousin had taken the church group and me to stand in front of the prison bars to talk, pray, and sing with the prisoners. We ended our visit by singing to the men in Creole a song about Jesus breaking every chain. To our surprise, virtually every man in the room responded by singing the words back to us in English. They told us, "It's a very good song."

What makes the exodus story so significant to me is its relevance to real life. Like many people of faith, I believe it shows how God intervenes in our lives to make them better. But even if you are skeptical about divine intervention, the story may inspire hope during unfavorable circumstances. Hope enables us to keep going, to believe that somehow things will get better—perhaps by a spiritual force, or our own efforts, or divine help underlying our efforts. Inspired by the exodus story, we may find ways to overcome our difficulties by changing our situation, or we may find ways to accept, at least for now, what cannot be changed. If we cannot change things immediately, we can still live with the hope that our struggles for freedom, fairness, and fulfillment will eventually succeed, and the longer the struggle, the more we need hope to get through our difficulties.

10

Celebrating a Peaceful Victory

How can you protect yourself and others while you struggle against abuse and injustice?

Exodus 6:2–7 (redemption of God's people);
12:1–13 (Passover), 29–30 (Egyptian deaths);
14:21–29 (crossing the sea); 15:1–21 (Song of the Sea)

Every time I saw Grandma, she took my picture. Years later, she explained why. She said my stepfather "would run around like a jackass" taking pictures of my half-sister and "never cared if you were in the picture or not." But Grandma's efforts were in vain. My mother later destroyed all the photo albums with pictures of me. She also stymied my grandparents' wish to leave a small legacy to me in their wills. Mom insisted that all the money should go to her and brought a lawyer to my grandparents' farm to change their wills.

Mom could not stand attention on anyone other than herself. When I got married after law school, I wanted a small wedding on my grandparents' farm, and I planned to cover any expenses. Grandma was thrilled to host the wedding. She immediately started sprucing up the farmhouse by replacing the dingy wallpaper room by room and repainting the chipped cabinets. But Mom put her foot down, demanding the wedding be held at her house. The idea repelled me because I had such bad memories of the two years I had lived there in high school. Still, my fiancé did not want to rock the boat, so I acquiesced.

Mom charged ahead, inviting people I had never met or hardly remembered. During the reception, one person after another told Mom how wonderful she and my stepfather had been to pay for my college and law school education. As she beamed at each of them, she never admitted that I had supported myself without parental help. After the wedding was over, my husband said, "We knew it would be bad. We just didn't know it would be this bad."

When we divorced some years later, I returned to the farm for a respite, stopping at my parents' house for a short visit along the way. My mother and stepfather barely acknowledged my presence because they were feuding by telephone with some relatives. Mom was so upset that she said she would kill herself and ran into the bedroom, as she had often done when I lived there. But this time my stepfather did not run after and plead with her as he had done in the past. He just sat there across from me at the kitchen table, his head down, saying he wished he were dead. Absent his overtures, Mom quickly returned to the kitchen. Then they went into another room to continue yelling over the phone at the relatives.

As I sat by myself at the kitchen table, I felt more convinced than ever before that my parents had nothing but misery to offer me, and as the prime target of their abuse, I was in the worst position of anyone to help them. Every time I tried to discuss my parents' mistreatment of me, Mom would scream and leave the room, and if I put my thoughts in a letter, she would refuse to read it. Now that she and my stepfather were not disparaging, hitting, molesting, or defrauding me, they had nothing else to say.

When I consider the despair I felt that day, the exodus story means more to me than any other story in the Bible. Just as the God of the exodus freed the Israelites, the story gives us hope that we may break out of oppressive situations. The Israelites never relied on unrealistic dreams of reconciliation with the Egyptians or debilitating efforts to forgive their slave masters. For people in troubled families, the story is a bold endorsement of leaving behind destructive relationships. Instead of living with misery, the exodus extols a victorious escape from torment. With great joy, it celebrates freedom from a lifetime of abuse.

THE BIBLE'S STORY

As described in Exodus 5:1, after Moses was called from the burning bush, he went to the pharaoh with this message from the God of Israel: "Let my people go." But the pharaoh refused to acknowledge Yahweh. The mighty deeds in the rest of the story convinced the Egyptians of Yahweh's power and caused the Israelites to affirm their belief.

As Moses learned in Exodus 6, God had made a sacred agreement called a covenant with Abraham, Isaac, and Jacob to give them the land of Canaan but had not made himself known to them by his name Yahweh.[145] After hearing the Israelites groan under Egyptian slavery, God remembered this covenant and wanted the Israelites to know: "I will free you from the burdens of the Egyptians and deliver you from slavery to them. I will redeem you with an outstretched arm and with great acts of judgment. I will take you as my people, and I will be your God."[146]

To convince the pharaoh to free the Israelites, God sent one plague after another against the Egyptians as told in Exodus 7–12. The waters of the Nile turned to blood; frogs, gnats, and flies successively swarmed the country; livestock died; people and animals festered with boils; hail, followed by locusts, destroyed the land; and the nation was covered in darkness. Still, the pharaoh refused to free the Israelites.

In Exodus 12, before the last plague struck the firstborn dead, God told Moses and his brother Aaron how to spare the Israelites. Each household took a lamb, slaughtered it at dusk, and put its blood on the doorframe of the house. That night the people roasted the meat over a fire and ate it along with bitter herbs reminiscent of slavery and unleavened bread made in haste without yeast so they could make a quick departure. In giving these instructions, God protected the Israelites from harm in what would become an annual ritual in remembrance of their departure. The ritual would bind the community together by reliving the experience in one generation after another.[147]

When God moved across Egypt to strike the firstborn, the Lord saw the lamb's blood as a sign of Israelite homes and passed over them. But every firstborn Egyptian male died, from the firstborn son of the pharaoh on the throne to the firstborn son of a prisoner in a dungeon to the firstborn son of a slave at her hand mill. Across the land there was loud wailing: someone had died in every Egyptian home. The plague was so terrifying that the pharaoh and his people drove the Israelites out of Egypt.

Shortly afterward, as told in Exodus 14, the pharaoh changed his mind and pursued the Israelites with his horses, chariots, chariot drivers, and army. When they cornered the Israelites against the sea, the Israelites were terrified. But Moses assured them, "[Yahweh] will fight for you."[148] Driving a strong wind, God parted the sea to let the Israelites walk through it on dry land, with the waters forming a wall to their right and to their left. As the pharaoh's horses, chariots, and chariot drivers pursued them, God clogged the chariot wheels. Then the sea returned to its normal depth and covered all the chariots and chariot drivers, along with the army following them. None of the Egyptians survived.

Moses and the other Israelites were ecstatic about their miraculous rescue from disaster. They praised God for their salvation in a victory hymn called Song of the Sea in Exodus 15:1–21. In the song, the Israelites proclaimed: "[Yahweh] is a warrior; [Yahweh] is his name."[149] They recited how Yahweh hurled into the sea horse and rider, chariots, and army, taking them down like stones and sinking them like lead. The hymn began with Moses and the Israelites singing to Yahweh about his glorious triumph, and afterward Miriam led the women with tambourines and dancing.

WRITING THE STORY

The dramatic deliverance of the Israelites from slavery shows how God intervenes to save people who are suffering. God did more than identify himself for the first time by his name Yahweh. He revealed a different aspect of divine nature: Yahweh was a warrior who fights for the oppressed.

From a historical perspective, the name Yahweh seemed to be first used to identify a local god far away from Israel's eventual homeland in Canaan. The name was originally known in the wasteland south and east of Canaan, inhabited by nomadic desert dwellers. Moses was around this area when God called him from a burning bush while he was tending the flock of his father-in-law, a Midianite priest. Quite a few other biblical passages, some of them going back to the oldest layers of the Bible, say Israel's God came from the same region. Aside from these passages, two temple inscriptions from around 1500 to 1000 BCE refer to nomads in this area as desert dwellers of Yahweh.[150]

In the passages that locate Yahweh in the region southeast of biblical Israel, his principal function at such time was warfare.[151] As a divine warrior, he fought for Israel on high while calling his people to fight on earth below. At least initially, he did not appear to be associated with sending life-giving rain during droughts, or assuring fertility, or providing other benefits for which ancient people turned to their gods. He was more focused on waging wars.

PART III | FINDING REDEMPTION

After the Israelite slaves arrived in Canaan, they described how Yahweh had rescued them in the poetic language of the Song of the Sea in Exodus 15. The archaic language of the poem suggests it is one of the oldest biblical passages, perhaps from the twelfth century BCE. Like other ancient biblical passages, the Song of the Sea extolled Yahweh's role as a divine warrior. The later narrative version of the sea crossing in Exodus 14 also described Yahweh as a divine warrior.[152]

To enhance Yahweh's role, both the sea-crossing narrative and poetic Song of the Sea drew on myths about the Canaanite god Baal. If the exodus occurred during the reign of Rameses II or Merneptah, the Israelites would have arrived in Canaan around the time Baal was usurping El as the supreme Canaanite god. El was considered the father of other gods, the creator of earth and people, and an old, wise, kindly father figure. Baal was a youthful, vigorous, powerful, and sometimes violent god who controlled the storm clouds and life-giving rain. Although both Baal and Yahweh were considered divine warriors, Baal was victorious in battling watery chaos often depicted as a sea monster. Instead of fighting cosmic battles with watery chaos, Yahweh fought for Israel in a historic sea battle against the pharaoh's army. The biblical writers changed Baal's battles with the cosmos into Yahweh's involvement in historical events to save Israel.[153]

During the Babylonian exile in the sixth century, the Israelites found inspiration in the exodus story because they again were living in a strange land and forced to work on its building projects. Although the exiles initially expected to be quickly rescued as portrayed in the Song of the Sea, they stayed in Babylon for more than five decades before a small group was allowed to return to Jerusalem. To help the exiles cope with this delay, Israelite writers apparently added the plagues to the exodus account. In these stories, God delayed rescuing the Israelite slaves to demonstrate divine power to the Egyptians and Israelites, and by implication, God would also deliver the exiles from Babylon even though it could take a long time.[154]

During the exile, Israelite writers also developed the Passover celebration in the exodus account. The festival was especially significant to the exiles because their traumatic survival during Jerusalem's destruction mirrored the survival of the Israelites during the Egyptian deaths. To celebrate Passover, exilic writers combined a festival of shepherds with a festival of farmers. In the springtime when sheep and goats were born, shepherds would sacrifice and eat an animal from their flock, assuring divine favor for the rest of the flock, and to ward off evil, they daubed the animal's blood on the doorframe of their houses. Around the same time of year, when the winter's barley crop was ready to harvest, farmers would celebrate by eating quickly prepared unleavened bread.[155]

Despite the joyful celebration of Passover, the exodus had a troubling undercurrent of violence. The rabbis recognized this when they considered the deaths of the Egyptian army in the sea. According to rabbinic commentary, the angels started to sing a hymn praising God as the Egyptians were drowning. But God rebuked them, saying, "While my creatures are drowning in the sea you would sing a hymn?!"[156] According to the rabbis, God showed that he does not rejoice in the death of the wicked.

LIVING BY THE STORY

God as a divine warrior is both an empowering and provocative image. We can take comfort in knowing God is on the side of the downtrodden in the fight for freedom and justice. This aspect of God offers us hope when we are mistreated and oppressed, and it encourages us to join the fight against injustice. But the destruction of the plagues and sea battle are sobering reminders of the high cost of battling for justice. If a peaceful solution in everyone's best interest is not practical, we need to guard against getting harmed as well as harming others.

From a political perspective, Josh and Ben, both Jewish men who told me how much Passover meant to them, illustrated this dilemma. Although each of them felt affinity for Israel, Josh focused on its security while Ben was concerned about its inequitable treatment of Arabs. In his view, the harm to Arabs contradicts the principles of social justice that made him proud to be Jewish. When Josh justified Israel's military operations to control terrorism, he was taken aback by Ben's response: "One person's terrorist is another person's freedom fighter."

Our personal struggles to overcome domestic violence and abuse can bring similar anguish. When Evelyn heard about my childhood experiences, she was eager to tell me of her own. As a child, she was repeatedly beaten by her mother. Then years later, to Evelyn's horror, she was so overcome by fury from the humiliation of past abuse that she hit her elderly mother while she was sitting in her wheelchair. Throughout Evelyn's life, she had been disparaged by her relatives, and after hitting her mother, she became the family's outcast.

PART III | FINDING REDEMPTION

Christine Ann Lawson, a clinical social worker, would understand Evelyn's rage toward her mother. Lawson wrote a book for adult children of abusive mothers with borderline personality disorders.[157] Such mothers often identify one child as bad, vent their rage by emotional and physical abuse of that child, and follow any gesture of compassion with another attack. The father frequently is dominated by but distant from the mother and does nothing to protect the child.

Lawson encourages adult children of abusive mothers to keep enough emotional and physical distance to prevent either the adult children or their mothers from turning to violence. In her view, no one should ever urge an adult abused as a child to continue a relationship with the abuser. For the adult child, she suggests these precautions: Never force yourself to get together with your parents; and if you do get together, keep the visit short, avoid being alone with them, do not expose vulnerabilities, stick to impersonal topics, and plan ahead for a quick exit if needed. Instead of dwelling on a troubled relationship, she says, build your own life, break the cycle of abuse with your own children, and avoid taking revenge against your parents.

Judith Herman, a Harvard Medical School professor who wrote a classic book on trauma, suggests a similar approach for battered spouses as well as adults who were abused as children.[158] Since adults in both groups often remain entangled in destructive relationships with their abusers, the key to recovery in her view is breaking free of these relationships. But freedom can be costly because of the loss of financial support from the abuser and the loss of family members and friends who take the abuser's side. A survivor needs the courage to provide for her own physical safety and economic well-being, to seek out relationships with trustworthy people, and to develop a more meaningful, expansive life.

Herman warns that the survivor's recovery from trauma will stagnate if she avoids facing the monumental loss caused by her abuse and diverts her attention instead to revenge or forgiveness.[159] While revenge clearly would be detrimental to both the survivor and abuser, transcending the rage and loss of trauma by forgiving the abuser at first glance seems appealing. But it is unlikely to be feasible for the survivor unless the abuser confesses, repents, and makes amends, which in Herman's view is "a rare miracle." She says that healing depends on discovering restorative love in the survivor's own life. It does not require extending this love to the abuser. After the survivor mourns the traumatic event and builds her own life, she may be surprised to find the abuser no longer interests her. She may even feel sorrow and compassion for the abuser. But Herman does not consider this disengaged feeling the same as forgiveness.

I feel Lawson and Herman know exactly what it was like to grow up with my mother and stepfather. Although by trial and error I came to the same conclusions as Lawson and Herman, I would have had an easier time if they had been there to guide me in my younger years. In contrast to some sermons I have heard about forgiveness, their advice is more attuned to the well-being of the abused.

When Clifton Black, a biblical theology professor at Princeton Theological Seminary, gave a talk at a local church a few years ago, I was eager to hear what he had to say about forgiveness. Based on his book about the Lord's Prayer, his talk considered the prayer's request to our heavenly father to forgive our debts as we forgive our debtors.[160] When I asked about repeated wrongs like parental or spousal abuse, his response was emphatic, "Get out." He explained, "God doesn't want anyone abused, harmed, or mistreated. If you're mistreated, get out. Forgiveness is for later."

At a later point, perhaps the abusers will repent, or the survivors will have the extraordinary grace to forgive people who show no remorse and continue to harm them. More likely, the survivors will feel the sorrow and compassion I felt toward my mother and stepfather but not the warmth of forgiveness or reconciliation.

After the visit to my parents' home where I sat alone at the kitchen table while they yelled at relatives over the phone, I went to their house only on limited occasions. Their vindictiveness and indifference were just too draining. When I told my grandparents my decision, I was overjoyed by their response. Even though they maintained a close relationship with my mother and stepfather, they fully supported me.

Picturing God as a divine warrior gives me a more multidimensional understanding of the exodus story's meaning for my life. Because I had always considered my grandparents' farm a safe haven, I readily linked the exodus to salvation by divine love expressed through my grandparents. When I thought about God as a divine warrior, I saw another aspect of the story. Given the detrimental effects of child abuse, I now imagine the warrior God helping me break free of the destructive relationship with my parents. Like the Israelites leaving Egypt, I left my parents' house for a better life, free of their abuse.

PART III | FINDING REDEMPTION

In our imperfect lives, I feel God wants us to seek a realistic approach to destructive relationships, whether by reconciling, staying on guard, or leaving. Reconciliation is possible only if the destructive party is able and willing to change. Staying on guard from the person who has harmed us may be a viable approach if we succeed at maintaining emotional distance and stopping unpleasant interactions. If staying on guard is draining or ineffective, leaving may be the best option. Under these circumstances, it can be an exhilarating experience of great joy.

11

Making It through the Wilderness

When you have overcome difficulties, how has it changed the way you see yourself, your life story, and your spiritual views?

Exodus 19:3–6 (Holy Nation); 20:1–17 (Ten Commandments)

I was near the top of Great-Grandpa's bucket list. He told me many times, "I hope I live long enough to see the day you become a lawyer." One of sixteen children, he went to a single-room country school through third grade. Then he bought the farm, married Great-Grandma, and raised Grandpa and his siblings. When I was in ninth grade, Great-Grandpa was delighted to hear I wanted to be a lawyer. He told me no one in our "entire relation" had ever been a lawyer.

Although Great-Grandpa died before I became an attorney, Grandpa, who like Grandma had an eighth-grade education, was just as proud. After I graduated from law school, Grandpa took me to the bar in town to ask each man sitting around the counter, "Have you met my granddaughter the lawyer?" When my grandparents and I went to a local restaurant on my next visit, Grandpa was wearing the hearing aids I had bought him with my first paychecks. He announced to all the people at the tables around us, "My granddaughter the lawyer bought me these hearing aids."

The encouragement of my relatives on the farm helped me through the grueling years after I left my parents' house before beginning my legal career. Given no money from my parents and inadequate financial aid from my college, paying for my education was an enormous struggle. One summer I pushed corn onto a conveyor belt at the canning factory near the farm from seven p.m. to seven a.m., seven days a week unless it rained. Another summer I worked as a playground leader on weekdays, a film processor on weeknights, and a waitress in a pancake house on Sundays. Exhausted, I pleaded again and again for more financial aid from the college. But my requests were denied by cynically explaining that giving me more money would cause other students to work long hours and claim parental abuse so they could get more money too.

My experiences are typical of the long and difficult period it often takes to overcome adversity. Leaving my parents' house was not enough. I needed to make sense of the hardships of my past and move beyond them. I had to see myself in a different light with a new way of life. To do this took grit and hard work along with the encouragement of people who believed in me and wanted me to succeed. By the time I established myself as an attorney, I was well on my way to a better future.

I appreciate the Israelites' journey through the wilderness because it highlights the difficulty of breaking free from bondage for a new life. After God rescued the Israelite slaves, they celebrated their release with unrestrained enthusiasm. But escaping slavery was just the first step of a radical transformation. Instead of seeing themselves as slaves, they needed to become God's people living God's way. The exodus story is not only about changing our physical location or circumstances; it is also about an inward change in who we are and how we see ourselves.

THE BIBLE'S STORY

As described in the book of Exodus, the redemption of the Israelite slaves led to an agreement called a covenant, which set the terms of God's special relationship with the Israelites. Prior to their deliverance, the Lord had told them in Exodus 6:7 the key aspects of this relationship: "I will take you as my people, and I will be your God." As God's chosen people, the Israelites would have a special obligation to carry out God's will and exemplify how to live God's way.

After the Israelites left Egypt, the Lord protected them on a harrowing journey through the wilderness to the foot of Mount Sinai. There, in Exodus 19, the Lord reminded them that he had borne them on "eagles' wings," an image of parental protection recalling an eagle training its young to fly, catching them on its back when they tire or fall.[161] If the Israelites obeyed the

Lord's voice, out of all the earth's people, they would be "a priestly kingdom and a holy nation." Like priests in the ancient world, every Israelite would be intimate with God and responsible for moral and physical purity.[162]

At Mount Sinai, the Lord gave the Israelites the Ten Commandments as the key stipulations of the covenant. Although the Bible refers to ten words or sayings, the commandments are not numbered. These are the Ten Commandments in Exodus 20:2–17 as they are numbered in many Protestant traditions:

> I am the LORD your God, who brought you out of the land of Egypt, out of the house of slavery;
> [1] you shall have no other gods before me.
> [2] You shall not make for yourself an idol, whether in the form of anything that is in heaven above or that is on the earth beneath or that is in the water under the earth. . . .
> [3] You shall not make wrongful use of the name of the LORD your God, . . .
> [4] Remember the sabbath day, and keep it holy. . . .
> [5] Honor your father and your mother, so that your days may be long in the land that the LORD your God is giving you.
> [6] You shall not murder.
> [7] You shall not commit adultery.
> [8] You shall not steal.
> [9] You shall not bear false witness against your neighbor.
> [10] You shall not covet your neighbor's house; you shall not covet your neighbor's wife, male or female slave, ox, donkey, or anything that belongs to your neighbor.[163]

The Ten Commandments are so essential that the Bible repeats them with some variation in Deuteronomy 5:6–21. They are like a constitution setting forth basic principles of the community. The belief that God provided the laws was a distinctive feature in the ancient Near East. Mesopotamian kings claimed to learn about truth and justice from the gods, but kings themselves declared the specific laws. In Israel, God took the place of a king and revealed the laws to everyone.[164]

After giving the Israelites the Ten Commandments, God spelled out the terms of the covenant in greater detail in the Covenant Code in Exodus 20:22—23:33. The code provides for religious, civil, and criminal matters enforced by financial compensation, capital punishment, and other consequences for violations. By contrast, the Ten Commandments are brief mandates and prohibitions that rely on God's authority and the people's obedience for enforcement.

After the Israelites' deliverance from bondage, the laws supported the profound transformation of the Israelites from slaves to God's people. The Israelites had a special relationship with the Lord, they were nurtured like a parent would nurture the young, and they were taught the best way to live. The Lord even told them how to build a wilderness tabernacle as an earthly home for the deity to dwell among them.

WRITING THE STORY

As told in the Bible, Mount Sinai was the dramatic setting where God established a covenant with the Israelites and gave them the Ten Commandments and Covenant Code. But the Israelites' understanding of the covenant and laws probably evolved after they reached Canaan during the tribal period and monarchy. Long after the events at Mount Sinai, the Israelites wrote down what had happened based on their understanding of these events in later years. If we look at how the covenant and laws developed over several centuries from a historical perspective, it helps us appreciate the profound transformation the Israelites made from slaves to God's people.

As a likely scenario, the escaped slaves from Egypt told the Canaanite residents about Yahweh's miraculous rescue, and the descendants of these slaves along with some Canaanites eventually became the Israelite tribes. As these tribes were forming, settlers built numerous small hilltop villages in the central highlands. The villagers may have left cities in the lowlands due to political turmoil, or they may have been semi-nomads who settled down as farmers. In either case, except for the escaped slaves, most of the villagers in the central highlands seemed to have come from other parts of Canaan.[165]

The villagers lived on a subsistence level by growing crops and raising a few sheep, goats, and other animals. Grandparents, their sons, their sons' wives, unmarried daughters, and dependents lived together with a few animals in a small house with a couple rooms. Individual houses were grouped together in compounds for extended families, and possibly all the people in a village shared some kinship ties. For defense against raids from nearby areas or foreign invaders, Israelites in one village occasionally banded together with other villagers in the same tribe. Faced with a military crisis, the villagers of multiple tribes joined together in a temporary military alliance under a leader who rose to the occasion.[166]

As the Bible itself indicates, tribal life without a king could be turbulent. Some tribes would refuse a call to arms when needed to fight a common enemy. Besides inadequate defense, no laws were accepted and enforced to maintain order among the tribes. Although kinship norms prevailed within a village, they did not extend beyond it. In an egregious case, a traveler was threatened with gang rape, and his concubine was gang-raped and died. Yet tribal groups were reluctant to support a king for military protection and civil order because kings demanded high taxes and drafted people for military and work projects.[167]

To solve these difficulties, tribal leaders may have turned to the warrior god Yahweh as their divine king.[168] In the absence of an earthly monarch, the Israelites' identity as Yahweh's people would have been a way to unite tribal groups. Yahweh could wage wars by fighting for his people and summoning them to battle. He could also declare laws that would extend minimal kinship obligations to a broader group. The selection of Yahweh by tribal chiefs as their king seems to be confirmed by a particularly ancient biblical verse in Deuteronomy 33:5: "There [thus] came to be a [divine] king in Jeshurun [Israel], when the heads of people gathered together, all the chiefs of Israel."[169]

Eventually the Israelites viewed their relationship to God as a covenant. This view was influenced by ancient Near Eastern treaties between a local king and a powerful foreign king. Upon dominating or conquering a country, the foreign king would recite how he had benefitted the country, demand exclusive loyalty, and extract tribute and other obligations. Like a foreign king from afar, the warrior god Yahweh seemed to come from the area around Mount Sinai, a long distance away from the hill country of Israelite tribes. Just as a foreign king recited how much he benefitted the weaker king's country, Yahweh reminded the Israelites how he had led them out of slavery to Israel. Although allegiance to only one god was unusual in the ancient Near East, Yahweh's demand that the Israelites worship no other gods was like the demand for exclusive loyalty made by a foreign king.[170]

Once the Israelites considered their relationship to God as a covenant, they made the Ten Commandments stipulations of the covenant. The Ten Commandments likely reflected straightforward, commonly accepted ethical standards of the tribal period. Their format also suggests their use for instruction. The short dictates were easy to memorize and could be readily recalled by individuals counting them on their fingers. Their key values, simple form, and easy memorization have made them a core part of the educational curriculum in synagogues and churches down to the present day.[171]

The Covenant Code seems to be a later stipulation of the covenant. While the Ten Commandments were sufficient for small, family-based settlements early in the tribal period, the Covenant Code addressed a settled society of farmers and herders. The code provided for a judicial system, non-Israelite residents, loans to the poor secured by property, and penalties for thieves breaking into houses. In addition, many laws in the Covenant Code resembled those in the ancient Mesopotamian Code of Hammurabi, and this code would have been more familiar to the Israelites after they formed a monarchy and had scribes in the royal court.[172]

As told in the Bible, the events at Mount Sinai were a dramatic revelation of divine power. From a historical perspective, the Israelites might have experienced a spiritual presence in more gradual ways during the tribal period and monarchy. They might have turned to Yahweh in the tribal period for help in resisting attacks and enforcing ethical standards. Eventually, they saw their relationship to God as a covenant, and they made the Ten Commandments stipulations of the covenant. Afterward, they added the Covenant Code to provide laws for a more settled society. When writing the biblical account, the Israelites reflected their understanding of these historical developments to portray a remarkable transformation from a life of slavery to a life close to God.

LIVING BY THE STORY

The transformation of the Israelites from slaves to God's people reminds me of the profound changes we need to make whenever we overcome adversity. To leave the past behind, we change the way we see ourselves, and our new identity becomes part of a new way of life. In this transformation, the spiritual views of our past life sometimes help us overcome adversity, but other times need revamping to empower us in our new life. In either case, the change in our circumstances is so dramatic that we often revise the way we tell the story of our lives. We update our life story to reflect our adverse experiences and how we have moved beyond them.

Judith Herman, the Harvard Medical School professor who wrote the classic book on trauma, describes the difficult path to recovery for adults who have been abused as children.[173] The guiding principle of recovery is restoring the power and control of the survivors. As the first steps, they free themselves from physical, emotional, and financial entanglements with their abusers, and they mourn the enormity of their loss so they can move on with their lives. After acknowledging their trauma, they are ready to develop a new self with new relationships, and if they decide to confront their families, they prepare for a response of fury or denial. As part of their recovery, they leave behind their faith to the extent it has been badly damaged by the betrayal of people of utmost significance to them. The survivors find instead a spiritual path that makes sense of moral guilt, undeserved suffering, and justice and order in the world. As they continue to heal, they integrate their trauma and recovery in an updated, optimistic version of their life story.

While Herman's approach applies to people who overcome abuse, a different approach is needed for people who want to stop abusing others. As a recovering alcoholic, my friend Hannah regretted her misguided affair with a married man, stopped drinking, and tried to help others find sobriety. Taking the twelve-step approach, she began by confessing that her life had become unmanageable, she was powerless over her addiction, and she surrendered her will to the care of a higher power. As she took a moral inventory, she reviewed the ways her addiction had harmed her family, friends, and co-workers and tried to make amends. In her view, she could not have made such drastic changes until her life had gone so far downhill that she "hit bottom." From this perspective, hitting bottom gave meaning to the years she had lost by drinking.[174]

The contrast between Hannah's story and Herman's approach is striking. While alcoholics are urged to surrender to a higher power, Herman encourages abuse victims to exercise greater control over their lives. Far from surrendering to a higher power, they need to reassess their religious beliefs given the tragedy they have suffered. While recovering alcoholics make amends for their mistreatment of family members, Herman advises abuse victims to decide whether to confront their abusive families and, if so, to prepare for an angry and evasive response. In contrast to recovering alcoholics who believe that hitting bottom is necessary before they are ready to turn around their lives, abuse victims are encouraged instead to mourn the enormous loss they have suffered.

Despite our different experiences, both Hannah and I have personal stories of recovering from adversity. When we found ourselves in adverse circumstances, we struggled to turn around our lives. During this struggle, a spiritual presence seemed to lift us up from our despair. But an approach that worked for one of us would not work for the other. We needed to find a path that met our individual needs for concrete steps to a more fulfilling life.

Most people are not abused or alcoholics. But everyone has times when they feel overcome by difficulties in their lives. They may be stymied by roadblocks to their education or career; devastated by a divorce or death; obsessed by a poor relationship with their in-laws or boss; betrayed by family, friends, or co-workers; guilt-ridden about their mistreatment of someone else; fearful of a life-threatening illness; or increasingly handicapped by old age.

In these situations, we may find inspiration in the story of the Israelites freed from bondage to make a better life for themselves. Sometimes we may feel a divine power helps us in the dramatic way the Israelites experienced at Mount Sinai. More often we may feel a spiritual presence helps us in the gradual ways the Israelites may have experienced during the tribal period and monarchy. Even if we are not religious, their experiences remind us of the kind of real-life problems we still hope to overcome by some combination of our own efforts, the help of others, and a force beyond ourselves.

That is why I like my grandmother's picture of an angel guiding the little girl across the broken bridge in the storm. It illustrates how we can get past the turbulence to become the person we are meant to be.

PART IV

Picturing the Promised Land

(Leviticus, Numbers, and Deuteronomy)

12

Drawing Close to God

When you are burdened by a troubled past, how do you find peace of mind with glimmers of joy?

LEVITICUS 16:1–34 (YOM KIPPUR OR DAY OF ATONEMENT);
26:40–45 (REPENTANCE DURING EXILE)

WHEN I PUT IN the code, the doors clicked open to the dementia unit in rural Minnesota where my Aunt Mary was staying. After Uncle Bill's death, she had moved into a senior residence, advancing from independent living to assisted living and now memory care. Since she was very lonely, I liked to stay in the facility's guest room for several days whenever I returned to Minnesota. This time I was back for a couple days over Easter.

As I walked into the dementia unit, Aunt Mary was slumped in a wheelchair that she had recently acquired after several falls. When I put my hand on her shoulder, she looked up, smiled, and said, "So you're here from New York." Then she introduced me by my name to the people sitting near her. It warmed my heart that she still remembered me.

After the greetings, I pushed Aunt Mary in her wheelchair into a private room for residents visiting with guests. We sat side by side in front of the window overlooking the lake where Great-Grandpa used to fish for bullheads that Grandma would fry for supper. Now and then, Aunt Mary and I talked about the blue jays flying between the trees, the robin landing on a rock, and the squirrels running around the tree trunks. In our secluded spot, with a heightened sense of mortality at the dementia unit

PART IV | PICTURING THE PROMISED LAND

for Easter weekend, I felt a divine presence stretching through all the turmoil and sweetness of our family saga and lingering over the sadness of the intractable problems with my parents. I was grateful that troubled families can find peace despite all the wrongs that have been inflicted. Aunt Mary in her own way seemed to find a similar peace. In the past, she had sometimes talked about hurts and slights that bothered her, but now she could not remember them.

That evening Aunt Mary and I went to the Easter concert in the reception area of the senior facility. Led by four singers and a pianist, Aunt Mary joined them in singing "Christ the Lord Is Risen Today." Despite her limited conversational ability, she seemed to know every word of the song. Back at the dementia unit, Aunt Mary was excited to tell her roommate about the beautiful Easter music. Sharing Aunt Mary's enthusiasm, her roommate had a touching response: "No matter what, you will always be my best friend."

The next day, I took Aunt Mary outside for a stroll in her new wheelchair. In the past, we had taken long walks around the farm and down the country roads, and when she had first moved into the senior facility, we had walked by the lake and into the town. After her condition deteriorated, we could walk only along the hallways of the senior facility, and eventually even that was difficult. But now the wheelchair gave us a new sense of freedom. Breaking away from the dementia unit, we went along the lake and all over town, just like we used to do. Aunt Mary was thrilled with our newfound freedom. "My," she said, "we're going so far."

At the end of my visit, I told Aunt Mary that I loved her, and she told me, "I love you too. Take care of yourself."

As I left the dementia unit, I was overwhelmed by the love, peace, and joy of Easter. Aunt Mary was locked inside a dementia unit, her mind and body were breaking down, and she faced impending death. Yet she was living with moments of great joy. She sang her long-time favorite hymns with gusto, enjoyed watching the birds and squirrels from her lakefront view, and delighted in our wheelchair escapade around the lake and town. Instead of dwelling on her troubles, she was best friends with her roommate and telling me to take care of myself.

At first my feelings upon leaving the dementia unit took me by surprise. I had often gone to services on Good Friday about Jesus reconciling a broken world through his crucifixion and then attended services on Easter

Sunday about renewed life through his resurrection. But I had not expected to experience this message with an aging aunt at a senior facility.

By studying the book of Leviticus, I gained a better understanding of how our religious rituals have evolved from ancient times to this day. As portrayed in Leviticus, the Israelites learned rituals to draw close to the divine by expressing their devotion and making amends for their shortcomings. These rituals kept changing over the time the Bible was written and afterward continued to change. Today we still find new ways to enact a spiritual dimension in our lives, sometimes when alone, sometimes with family and friends, and sometimes in congregations. That Easter weekend I felt a sacred presence by savoring every moment of joy and tranquility with Aunt Mary.

THE BIBLE'S STORY

The priests who wrote Leviticus incorporated traditional religious practices of the ancient Near East and adapted them to meet the needs of the Israelites. The culmination of these practices was the observance of Yom Kippur, often called the Day of Atonement, the holiest day of the year to Jews. These practices influenced how people writing the New Testament understood Good Friday and Easter, and they continue to influence how we develop rituals that reflect our evolving notions of the sacred.

Before Leviticus begins, the Israelites had already built a portable sanctuary for God to dwell in their midst during their journey to the promised land. To the priests writing the book, God was a majestic, absolute ruler living in splendor and tranquility. Such splendor could be disrupted by moral sins as well as by physical impurities of the Israelites. For example, even though contact with a dead body, genital discharges, and skin diseases were not sinful, such contacts sometimes required bathing, laundering, purification offerings, and other action. If the Israelites committed moral sins or had physical impurities, such conduct could pollute the sanctuary, which could cause dreadful consequences for the Israelites. To prevent such consequences, the priests taught the people how to avoid defiling the sanctuary, and the priests purged it whenever it had been defiled.[175]

To draw closer to God, the Israelites could take animal or other sacrifices to the sanctuary. Leviticus 1:1—3:17 permits voluntary sacrifices as gifts that convey love and reverence. Like our prayers today, these sacrifices might have been intended to express devotion, request help in distress, or show gratitude for escaping danger or harm. By contrast, Leviticus 4:1—6:7 requires offerings to "atone" (in Hebrew *kippur*) for specific violations or wrongdoing. We sometimes assume atoning means making amends for wrongdoing in order to be reconciled with God. But literally, the Hebrew term means "wipe clean." The blood of the animal would be used to cleanse the sanctuary by ritually purging it of contamination.[176]

As described in Leviticus 16, Yom Kippur provided another safeguard in the fall of each year. The Israelite high priest would sacrifice a bull to atone for his household and a goat to atone for the people. Then he would sprinkle the blood of the bull and goat to atone for the sanctuary itself. Finally, he would lay both his hands upon the head of a second goat, confess over it all the sins of the Israelites, and put their sins on the goat's head. After that, the goat would be sent away to carry their intentional sins into the wilderness. Although deliberate wrongs could never be undone, they could be sent away in the hope that they would never return.[177]

Besides purifying the sanctuary, Yom Kippur brought spiritual renewal to the entire Israelite community. As provided in Leviticus 16:29–34 and 23:26–32, the holiday gave people confidence that their relationship with God had been restored by cleansing them of their sins. To participate in the holiday, they stopped working and denied themselves food and drink. As additional forms of self-denial, rabbis in later years prohibited washing, wearing leather shoes, and engaging in sex.[178]

But sacrifices were not the only path to forgiveness. Leviticus 26:40–45 suggests another approach for the Babylonian exiles. If they humbled themselves, confessed their sins, and made amends, God would remember his covenant with Abraham. After they committed themselves to complying with divine commands, the slate would be wiped clean of accumulated guilt.[179]

This passage is one of the latest additions to Leviticus. After the book was finalized, Jews continued to adapt religious rituals to their evolving understanding of their relationship with God, and Christians considered the text when developing their understanding of God in light of Jesus Christ. These religious practices also affect the personal rituals we develop for ourselves and our families outside of synagogues or churches.

WRITING THE STORY

Much of Leviticus appears to have been written by priests in Jerusalem before the Babylonian exile and then revised during or after the exile.[180] These priests were carrying on an ancient tradition in the Near East. From early times, a temple had been considered the house of a god or goddess. If priests properly served the deity by animal sacrifices and other means, the deity looked out for the prosperity and success of the city associated with the temple.[181]

To purge the temple, Israelite priests adapted customary Near Eastern rituals. Like the Israelite high priest, a Babylonian priest would enter the sanctuary, use the body of a slaughtered ram in a ritual to purge the temple, and then use the ram's head in another ritual in the open country. In Israel, Yom Kippur may have begun as a similar ritual to purge the temple whenever it had been defiled and later became an annual event.[182]

A group of Israelite priests known as the holiness school eventually expanded Yom Kippur to a community-wide event involving forgiveness of sins. While the Israelite priests traditionally focused on the holiness of the priests and sanctuary, the holiness school was concerned about the holiness of all the Israelites and the entire land of Israel. The school added the passages in Leviticus 16:29–34 and 23:26–32 that provided for cleansing people of their sins and required them to fast and stop work. Instead of focusing on purging the temple, the updated ritual included the participation and forgiveness of all the Israelites.[183]

The holiness school made another significant contribution during the Babylonian exile. At that time, sacrifices were temporarily halted because of the destruction of the temple in Jerusalem. To deal with this contingency, the holiness school added the passages in Leviticus 26:40–45 that allowed the exiles simply to confess their sins to restore their relationship with God.[184]

Although sacrifices resumed after the exiles returned to Jerusalem and rebuilt the temple, Rome's destruction of the rebuilt temple in 70 CE stopped them entirely. Long before then, according to Jewish tradition, Abraham had asked God what would happen to the Israelites without a temple, and God had responded, "Whenever they read about the sacrifices I shall consider them as having offered sacrifices in My Presence, and I shall forgive them all their sins."[185] Since the temple's destruction, Yom Kippur has included readings from Scripture about sacrifices rather than the sacrifices themselves.

Even so, the temple's destruction led to a change in emphasis from sacrifices to repentance. Although the rite of confession had been only a small element of Yom Kippur, it soon became its central feature. In the days leading up to Yom Kippur, people were urged to repair relationships because atonement depended on righting wrongs. Although Yom Kippur atoned for sins between the people and God, it atoned for sins between one person and another only if the offender had reconciled with the aggrieved.[186]

While Jews were reconsidering the meaning of sacrifices given the temple's destruction in 70 CE, early Christians were reconsidering the meaning of sacrifices given Jesus's death in 30 CE. Yom Kippur as described in Leviticus strongly influenced the understanding of his death in the book of Hebrews in the New Testament. Hebrews 2:17 calls Jesus a "high priest in the service of God, to make a sacrifice of atonement for the sins of the people." According to Hebrews 9:22, his death was crucial to divine forgiveness because "without the shedding of blood there is no forgiveness of sins." The apostle Paul was also influenced by Leviticus when he wrote the book of Romans in the New Testament. He said God redeemed us by putting forth Jesus Christ as "a sacrifice of atonement by his blood, effective through faith," which saves us because "we have now been justified by his blood."[187]

Salvation through faith had a powerful impact on Paul and the Christian community. Even when Paul was in prison facing political and religious opposition, suffering, and death, he talked about the great joy he experienced. He urged others not to worry, for "the peace of God, which surpasses all understanding, will guard your hearts and your minds in Christ Jesus."[188] However different the circumstances, Paul's assurance resonated with me after my visit with Aunt Mary. She was imprisoned in a dementia unit where she and her companions were deteriorating and would die. Yet she found great beauty in the Easter hymns, shared their beauty with others, and enjoyed a temporary release from confinement during our excursion around the lake and town. Paul's message seemed to explain how the peace of God, surpassing all understanding, had guarded her heart and mind.

LIVING BY THE STORY

After I studied Leviticus, I felt empathy for the Israelites taking animal sacrifices to draw closer to God. Since those days, both Judaism and Christianity have transformed the meaning of sacrifices. Yet we still look for rituals to express our deepest spiritual concerns.

To my friend Elizabeth, Jesus's sacrificial death was key to Easter. As a lifelong Catholic, she agreed with the church's doctrine that his crucifixion and resurrection had conquered sin and death. In her view, the crucifixion had to be bloody: "When you look at all the terrible things people do to each other, there is a lot to be redeemed. If Christ suffered and died for all the sins of humanity, it had to be gory."

Elizabeth admitted that a bodily resurrection is not important to her. Yet she believed that Jesus brings new life through his resurrection. As she said, "By living close to Christ, we can experience eternal life even now," and she hoped that her "spirit will live in peace and bliss throughout eternity." To her, the drama of the Easter service underscores its basic message: "God loves us and calls us to love others."

My friend Ben dismissed sacrifices as a historical relic and seldom went to synagogue on Yom Kippur. But he still viewed the holiday as a time for reflection, beginning ten days earlier on Rosh Hashanah, the Jewish New Year. He appreciated the period of introspection and repentance starting on Rosh Hashanah and leading up to Yom Kippur. "It's like going back to school in the fall," he said. "It puts you in a different frame of mind. Maybe you'll apologize for something you've done, and maybe you'll be a little nicer."

When Ben recently obliged his mother by accompanying her to a Yom Kippur service, he was amazed by the power of repentance. At first the service brought back memories of what he called "self-affliction." As he described it, "You pray your butt off. You keep standing up and sitting down, and don't forget, you haven't had any food or water, you can't wash or shave, and you can't wear leather shoes." Yet he found the ritual surprisingly moving. The more he repented of his sins along with other congregants, the closer he felt to God. As he explained, "The gates of prayer are especially open that day. It's your best shot to reach God and God to reach you. In the end you have divine forgiveness." He quickly added, "We don't literally believe the gates of prayer open and shut." Still, he found his "heart was in it when standing, fasting, and repenting by the gates of prayer."

I had not expected to celebrate the Jewish holidays when my friend Olivia invited me to kayak with her on a lake in a state park outside of New York City. After a Christian upbringing, Olivia had converted to Judaism upon her marriage to a Jewish man. When they divorced, she lost interest

PART IV | PICTURING THE PROMISED LAND

in churches and synagogues and found meditation and nature more conducive to spirituality. On the drive to the lake, she told me it was Rosh Hashanah, and she practiced a Jewish custom every year on that day. Following this custom, she would throw breadcrumbs onto a lake to symbolize that she was casting away sin. After we kayaked to a secluded inlet along the lake, she read a meditation, and we threw breadcrumbs into the water. In the silence of the woods, it felt incredibly peaceful to sit still in our kayaks with the waves lapping gently against them.

After studying Leviticus, I regard Yom Kippur and Easter as part of a continuing quest to experience a spiritual dimension in life in ways that fit our changing circumstances. When Aunt Mary and I joined this quest, we no longer dwelled on wrongs of the past. It was enough to know that all had been forgiven. Now was the time to savor the remaining moments of joy. Our wheelchair trip around the town symbolized to me the freedom and exuberance of renewed life.

13

Blessings for the Journey

In trying circumstances, how do you stay calm enough to approach life with courage rather than fear?

NUMBERS 6:22–27 (BENEDICTION); 13:1—14:38 (SPY MISSION)

O NE OF MY FAVORITE passages in the Bible is known as the priestly blessing in Numbers 6:24–26: "The LORD bless you and keep you; / the LORD make his face to shine upon you and be gracious to you; / the LORD lift up his countenance upon you and give you peace." Whenever I feel troubled, I remember this benediction, often recited at church and synagogue services just before the congregation returns to daily life. No matter how anxious I feel, when I recite this blessing, it becomes a mantra that soothes the worries that keep me from moving forward.

Since ancient times, the priestly blessing has been an antidote to fear. The oldest actual copy of a biblical text is the inscription of this passage on silver jewelry in a burial cave near Jerusalem.[189] The piece dates to just before the city fell to the Babylonians around 586 BCE. Its residents apparently found solace in the blessing while their enemy threatened the city's destruction.

As described in Numbers, when the priests pronounced the blessing, it safeguarded the Israelites from dangers that threatened their way of life. By trusting in the Lord, they were assured of divine protection. They could overcome their fear of an arduous journey and reach the promised land.

PART IV | PICTURING THE PROMISED LAND

Like the Israelites, we often waver between trust and mistrust, courage and fear, hope and despair. If we have confidence in a divine force that assures our well-being, we may find the strength to live our lives more fully, and even if we are skeptical about a power beyond ourselves, we still need a sense of trust, courage, and hope for our journey through life.

THE BIBLE'S STORY

Numbers portrays a life of faith as a rite of passage that required the Israelites to follow God through the wilderness to the promised land.[190] At the beginning of the book, the Israelites were still near Mount Sinai, making final preparations for their journey to Canaan. The Lord told them to take a census (hence the book's name Numbers), counting the men in each tribe who were at least twenty years old and able to go to war against the people then living in Canaan. During the difficult journey through the wilderness, the generation counted in the first census failed to put their trust in the Lord. By the end of the book, that generation had died, a more faithful younger generation stood on the edge of the promised land, and another census counted the men of that generation able to go to war.

To prepare for the journey, the Lord instructed Moses and his brother Aaron to put the Israelites' camp around the sanctuary where God's presence dwelt. That way, God's holiness would pour out of the sanctuary throughout the camp. Aaron as the high priest and his sons performed the duties of priests, and other members of the Levite tribe protected the sanctuary and performed services for it. The other tribes were arranged around the camp and learned the purity and ethical requirements that would avoid defiling the camp and driving away God.

After the Israelites were given these instructions, the Lord said Aaron and his sons should pronounce on the Israelites my much-loved blessing described in Numbers 6:22–27. Each line of the blessing has one verb describing God's action toward the Israelites (bless, shine, lift) and another describing the results of that action (keep, be gracious, give peace). The wording suggests that God will bless the Israelites with security, soften his judgment with mercy, and care for the fullness of their lives. Each line is longer than the previous one, offering hope for an ever-expanding blessing. As conveyed by the blessing, God is protective of individuals peacefully living satisfying lives in a community.[191]

Blessings for the Journey

At the start of the journey in Numbers 10:11, the Lord's guidance and blessing would seem to guarantee the Israelites' success. But they soon became disgruntled. They complained about the food, violated divine commands, and rebelled against their leaders and the Lord. Even Moses and Aaron failed to follow the Lord's instructions for bringing water out of a rock and consequently were barred from entering the promised land.[192]

In Numbers 13:1–14:38, a mission to spy on the land and the people of Canaan illustrates how fear overtook trust in God. On the Lord's command, twelve scouts, one from each tribe, conducted surveillance across Canaan. Moses told the scouts to see whether the people were many or few, strong or weak; whether the towns were fortified or without walls; and whether the land had trees and was rich or poor. He added that the scouts should bring back some fruit.

For forty days, the scouts explored Canaan to evaluate the land throughout the region and to survey the southern border in preparation for conquest. When they returned to Moses and the other Israelites, the scouts said that the land flowed with "milk and honey," bringing back figs, pomegranates, and a cluster of grapes so large that two men carried it on a pole. But the scouts warned that the Canaanites were strong, their cities were large and fortified, and the people included a race of frightening giants.

Even so, Caleb urged the Israelites to occupy the land because they could overcome it. But the other scouts warned that the Israelites could not prevail because the Canaanites were stronger. These scouts claimed that the land devoured its residents and that the people were of such great size that "to ourselves we seemed like grasshoppers, and so we seemed to them."[193]

Upon hearing this, the Israelites were so distressed that they wished they had died in Egypt or the wilderness. They questioned why the Lord was taking them to a land to fall by the sword, and they said their wives and children would become booty. They decided to choose a captain and go back to Egypt.

Only Joshua joined Caleb and urged the Israelites to take over the land in reliance on God's protection. The other Israelites threatened to stone them. The Lord asked Moses how long the people would despise their God regardless of all that had been done for them, and the Lord threatened to destroy the people with a pestilence, disinherit them, and make Moses and his descendants a great nation. In response, Moses said that if the Israelites were destroyed, other nations would claim the Lord was not powerful enough to bring the Israelites to the land, and Moses urged the Lord to reveal his power by the love and mercy previously shown the Israelites.

God was still disappointed that the Israelites distrusted the divine promise of land even though the Lord had liberated them from slavery and taken care of them in the wilderness. As a consequence, except for Caleb and Joshua, the older generation died wandering in the wilderness for forty years, one year for each day of the spy mission. During this period, instead of being taken as booty, the younger generation forged a new identity more responsive to the Lord.

At the conclusion of Numbers, led by Joshua, the younger generation of Israelites was on the edge of the promised land about to enter Canaan.

WRITING THE STORY

By developing priestly, scribal, and other sources, the Israelite priests apparently shaped Numbers to envision a new life for the Israelites upon their return to Jerusalem from their exile in Babylon.[194] After the Persians conquered Babylon, they permitted some exiles to go home and rebuild their temple. Upon its completion, an era of temple-centered Judaism began. Like the priesthood portrayed in Numbers, the high priest gained authority, the priesthood was limited to descendants of Aaron, and other Levites had a subordinate religious role. Although some biblical passages suggest that all the descendants of Jacob's son Levi were once considered priests, after the exile, a power struggle seemed to limit priests to descendants of Aaron.[195] Hopes for a monarchy never materialized.

Faced with catastrophic losses suffered in the Babylonian and previous Assyrian invasions, the Israelite exiles blamed their forefathers' sins rather than doubt the power of their God. To rectify the past, the exiles hoped to become "a priestly kingdom and a holy nation" in the words of Exodus 19:6. The Hebrew word for holiness, *qadash*, means separate, suggesting people separated from others for God. The concept acquired special significance during the exile because the Israelites stayed in separate communities in previously vacated parts of Babylon. To maintain their identity, they practiced purity requirements once limited to priests, and they emphasized religious practices like the Sabbath and Passover that did not require a temple.[196]

The Israelite exiles were forced to stay in Babylon more than fifty years before some of them were allowed to return to Jerusalem. During that time, the first generation of exiles died, and only their children were able to return to the city. When they left Babylon, they wanted to make sure they maintained their religious standards. Although Israelite royalty, priests, administrators, and craftspeople had been marched to Babylon, the poor of the land had been left behind in Jerusalem. When the exiles finally returned to the city, the poor of the land seemed like strangers with immoral values and religious practices. The returning exiles considered their very survival dependent on retaking the land and resisting the sinful lifestyle of the local population.[197]

To inspire the exiles returning to Jerusalem, the Israelite priests writing Numbers described how the purity instructions and blessing had protected the freed slaves traveling from Egypt to the promised land. As told by the priests, before the slaves left for the promised land, God provided instructions to maintain purity and prevent defilement of the Israelite camp during the journey. At the end of these instructions, the priests wrote about Aaron and his sons blessing the Israelites in the ancient words of my much-loved blessing. Its placement at the end of the purity instructions suggested that it would safeguard the Israelites against defilement by infusing the camp with the power of the divine blessing.[198]

To emphasize to the exiles the significance of trusting in the Lord, the Israelite priests described how the spy mission in Numbers had resulted in the death of the older generation while they wandered in the wilderness for forty years. By mirroring the generational turnover of the Israelite exiles in Babylon, the priests' account suggested that the Lord would return the Israelite exiles to their homeland even if it took longer than expected, and the account showed the disastrous consequences of lacking enough trust to embrace God's promise of the land and return to it.[199]

In final form, Numbers highlights the tension between trust in God and anxiety about the future. The blessing before the start of the wilderness journey infused them with divine power to stay close to the Lord and assure their well-being. Yet the Israelites were stymied by fear, as dramatized by the spy mission. They could not reach the promised land unless they put their trust in the Lord.

LIVING BY THE STORY

When reading Numbers, we can relate to ways in which the Israelites' trust in the Lord was key to the rite of passage leading to the promised land. These days we may not expect trust in God to solve every problem or mistrust to result in death, and we may have misgivings about waging war against the Canaanites to take their land. Yet we still recognize an essential point of the story. If we trust in a spiritual power or other force for goodness, our worries, anxieties, and fears are less likely to hold us back from living life to the fullest.

In *Childhood and Society* and related works, Eric Erikson explains how basic trust helps us approach life with courage rather than fear.[200] In discussing our life journey, he considers trust the foundation of our personal development. In the life of an individual, trust begins with the comfort and familiarity of a parent responding to an infant's needs, and through this interaction, the infant feels safe and secure. By developing trust, we become more open to experience by gaining confidence in a positive outcome. If instead we have relentlessly negative or insecure experiences during our first year of life, mistrust may color our view of the world. Even then, a change for the better in our social conditions sometimes overcomes mistrust, or we may find within us the psychological strength and resilience to prevail.

Erikson associates trust with hope buttressed by faith. He finds that religions provide a social context that reinforces optimism. In his view, all religions encourage a childlike surrender to a provider of earthly fortune and spiritual health, the admission of misdeeds and evil intentions, and the restoration of faith in the goodness of our striving and the kindness of the powers of the universe. When things do not go well, religious sentiment helps people restore hope by engaging in prayer and other rituals. These rituals remind us of a spiritual force that assures us that we are not alone and that everything will turn out all right.

As Erikson describes our life journey, even though we cannot avoid death, we can overcome fear of death. In the last stage of life, we learn to appreciate our individual life as a specific part of a grand sequence of historical events. In doing so, we place our unique life within a broader context of world order and spirituality. By valuing our life in this context, we ease our anxiety as we near death, and we avoid feeling despair over a wasted life.

Like prayer and other rituals, the priestly blessing in Numbers seems to help us through our personal struggles. It may give us hope to rise above unfavorable experiences in our childhoods and to calm our worries during stressful times as adults. For me, the blessing has been especially important when anxiety holds me back from doing what I want to do. It seems to build the confidence sometimes battered in my childhood. For my friend

Elizabeth, the blessing has meant the most after the death of a loved one. It helps her experience her sorrow in the context of a much greater religious framework. When hearing the blessing at burial services for friends and relatives, she calls it "a beautiful passage at times of grief."

We all want comfort during our difficulties and hope for a better future. For many people, these simple words of the priestly blessing seem to have a transcendent power to instill calm in chaos: "The Lord bless you and keep you; / the Lord make his face to shine upon you and be gracious to you; / the Lord lift up his countenance upon you and give you peace."

14

Centering Our Lives

What moves you to center your life on God or whatever has utmost significance to you?

DEUTERONOMY 6:1–9 (SHEMA OR GREAT COMMANDMENT)

WHILE I STOOD IN the hallway outside my grandparents' bedroom, I worried that something terrible was about to happen. During the past year in grade school, Grandma's ulcers had made her sick, and now the doctors wanted to remove part of her stomach. After Grandpa told me to wait in the hall that day, I watched the grown-ups go in and out of the bedroom, speaking in hushed tones. Everyone seemed scared about the surgery, yet no one would talk about it, which to me meant Grandma might die.

Right before my grandparents left for the hospital, Grandpa told me to go into the bedroom, and Grandma asked the other people in the room to leave so she could speak to me alone. When I entered the room, she was lying pale and weak against the white sheets. She told me to sit down on her bed and took my hand. Then she asked me to promise that I would always believe in Jesus. As I made this solemn oath, I knew how much Jesus meant to her, and I wanted to do whatever she asked to show I loved and honored her. But I did not make this promise just for her sake. I felt she wanted me to count on Jesus so I would have a better life.

Although Grandma lived for many more decades, I still marvel at her clear-sightedness before her operation. Back then, she did not know whether she would return home or who would look out for me. She could have told me how much I meant to her, or she could have given me guidance on the best way to live, or she could have assured me that everything would work out well. Instead, she focused like a laser beam on Jesus. She knew I would be fine if I put my trust in the Lord.

In subsequent years, I learned that the biblical book of Deuteronomy advocates Grandma's approach. The book tells us to make God the center of our lives, and if we do, it assures us that everything else will fall into place. It considers this message so important that each generation must teach it to the next. To do so, the book itself shows us how to reach the heart of the next generation and make sense as the culture changes. Such an approach is especially critical given the skepticism and individualism of our age.

THE BIBLE'S STORY

Deuteronomy is set on the border of the promised land. God already had rescued the Israelites from slavery and given them the Ten Commandments at Mount Sinai. But now the older generation had died, and a new generation would be continuing the journey.

Before entry into the promised land, Moses gave a series of motivational talks on how the Israelites should live in their long-awaited home. After reminding them that God had liberated them from slavery, Moses repeated with some variations the Ten Commandments, and he added other laws for their community. By living the way God intended, Moses said, they would find the source of life and well-being; otherwise, they would face destruction.

Even though the generation that escaped slavery had died, the new generation was treated as if God had saved them from bondage and given them the Ten Commandments. Moses urged them to pass along their story so that later generations could relive the experience and commit themselves to the Lord. In response, all the Israelites—men, women, and children—stood before the Lord to enter a covenant that supplemented the covenant previously sworn at Mount Sinai.[201]

At the core of the book, Deuteronomy 6:4–5 affirms that God is the center of life: "Hear, O Israel: The LORD is our God, the LORD alone. You shall love the LORD your God with all your heart and with all your soul and with all your might." In Jewish tradition, these words begin the prayer called the Shema, the Hebrew word for "hear." In Christian tradition, these lines are known as the Great Commandment. When Jesus was asked which commandment was first of all, he said that the entire divine law hung on the Great Commandment along with a second commandment from Leviticus 19:18 to "love your neighbor as yourself."[202]

Love of God and neighbor did not mean simply personal feelings, emotions, or beliefs. The Israelites were expected to express their love by their conduct, and their conduct involved their heart, soul, and might. Heart meant what we now consider both the heart and the mind. Soul meant the vital life strength infusing an entire person and empowering desire, thought, will, and movement. Might meant power or strength, emphasizing the force of loving the Lord. To the Israelites, such love was a stance of loyalty and devotion to a divine being far greater than themselves.[203]

Following the Shema, Deuteronomy 6:6–9 urges the Israelites to keep the Lord's commands in their hearts. To internalize them, they should: "Recite them to your children and talk about them when you are at home and when you are away, when you lie down and when you rise." As reminders, they should wear the commands on their bodies and inscribe them on their doorways and gates.

While emphasizing Israel's relationship with God, Moses made the clearest statement of monotheism in the Bible's first five books. In Deuteronomy 4:39, he told the Israelites that "the LORD is God in heaven above and on the earth beneath; there is no other." Although the Ten Commandment and the Shema demand exclusive allegiance to Israel's God, they do not deny the existence of other deities. After monotheism became the dominant view in religious circles, the Ten Commandments and Shema were reinterpreted to affirm God's greatness as the sole God in heaven and earth.[204]

WRITING THE STORY

Although Deuteronomy tells the ancient story of the exodus, it tells the story in a new way to a new generation. For several centuries, the Israelites had been besieged by foreign powers. During that time, the Israelites questioned whether their God was still powerful and loyal to them. In response to their concerns, Deuteronomy initially urged exclusive devotion to Yahweh and eventually recognized Yahweh as the sole God of heaven and earth.

As the Bible reports in 2 Kings 22, an early version of Deuteronomy was discovered in Jerusalem's temple around 622 BCE during King Josiah's reign.[205] The original text may have been written in Israel's northern region when it was dominated by the Assyrians and then taken to Jerusalem after the northern region was destroyed by the Assyrians in 722 BCE. The text's emphasis on loyalty to Yahweh suggests the influence of the Israelite prophet Hosea. While living in the northern region during Assyrian domination, he had reassured the Israelites that Yahweh loved them as a husband loves his wife and wanted their exclusive devotion. But like a promiscuous wife with other lovers, Hosea said, Israel had pursued other gods, and Yahweh had used Assyrian oppression to bring his wayward wife back to him.[206]

Although the Assyrians dominated Jerusalem for many years after the northern region was destroyed, Assyrian power had waned by the time the early text of Deuteronomy was discovered during King Josiah's reign. After that discovery, King Josiah led reforms to assert Jerusalem's independence from the Assyrians by extending his authority into the northern region, destroying statues of foreign gods, and closing sanctuaries outside of Jerusalem. His reforms were attributed to the discovery of the early text along with its expansion by scribes in Jerusalem.[207]

In writing Deuteronomy, the scribes used the terms of a customary treaty of an Assyrian king with a subordinate state, but they applied the terms to God instead of to the Assyrian king.[208] When the Assyrians dominated a country, they made a covenant known as a vassal treaty that required the other country to "love" their king. Loving the king did not mean passion or intimacy. The term referred to political loyalty. The subordinate state expressed loyalty by solely serving the king with no allegiance whatsoever to any other power. The treaty began by describing what the king had done for the subordinate state, demanded exclusive loyalty to the king, and added specific obligations such as giving him money, providing troops, turning in traitors, and avoiding alliances with other nations. To enforce these obligations, the treaty provided blessings for obedience and curses for disobedience.

By adapting the terms of a treaty, Deuteronomy changed the way the Israelites saw God. Their scribes took the language of a treaty and applied it to "loving" God as described in the Ten Commandments and Shema.[209] Instead of recalling what the Assyrian king had done for the Israelites, Deuteronomy recalled what God had done, delivering them from bondage and giving them land. Instead of loving the Assyrian king by their loyalty and obedience, they expressed their love by devotion to God alone, complying with divine teachings and laws. As indicated by blessings for obedience and curses for disobedience, their entire well-being depended on devoting themselves to the Lord.

If a treaty imposed by a superpower had been the only model, Deuteronomy might have been an austere book of rigid demands. To embed its values on the hearts and minds of the Israelites, the scribes incorporated the educational methods, wisdom tradition, and love language of the ancient Near East. The Shema begins with "Hear, O Israel," which was a wisdom teacher's call for attention. Then the text instructs the Israelites to internalize the Lord's commands by reciting them to their children, talking about them wherever they are, and writing them on their surroundings. To describe the love of God, the scribes used language suggestive of lovers in ancient poetry and the love of Yahweh in Hosea.[210]

After King Josiah's reign, major developments on the political front changed the view of God reflected in previous versions of Deuteronomy. First the Babylonians destroyed Jerusalem and exiled the Israelites to Babylon, and then the Persians conquered Babylon and permitted the Israelites to return to Jerusalem. The biblical book of Isaiah suggested that God had sent foreign invaders to punish the Israelites for their sins and afterward sent the Persians to redeem them from exile. The text proclaimed that only one God exists, and this deity alone created the world and brings redemption. These passages from Isaiah are the earliest statements of monotheism in the Bible.[211]

Consistent with these passages in Isaiah, during or after the exile, Israelite editors of Deuteronomy added passages about only one God in heaven and earth, and religious leaders later reinterpreted the Shema and Ten Commandments to mean solely one God. After the Israelites returned to Jerusalem, belief in a single universal God became so widespread that the idea of multiple deities no longer made sense to them.[212]

In writing Deuteronomy, the scribes valued tradition yet related it to the political events and culture of their era. Parents were urged to tell their children the ancient story of the exodus and commandments. But the way parents would tell the story was influenced by the treaties and conduct of foreign nations and the wisdom tradition, educational methods, and love language of the ancient Near East. The Israelites would worship Yahweh as they had done for many centuries. But now they stressed worshiping solely Yahweh to the exclusion of other gods, they broadened their understanding of Yahweh in comparison with an Assyrian king, and they eventually realized Yahweh was not just their God but the sole God of heaven and earth.[213]

LIVING BY THE STORY

Like the scribes writing Deuteronomy, we face the challenge of telling the ancient biblical stories in a new way to a new generation. Instead of foreign powers and their gods calling into question the Israelites' faith, our views are more likely to be influenced by our secular culture with its emphasis on individual freedom. When we tell the biblical stories, we need to show that they still make sense in our society, and we need to do so in a way that reaches the heart of the next generation. In doing so, families have a critical role, just as Deuteronomy suggested.

As noted by sociologists Christian Smith at the University of Notre Dame and Amy Adamczyk at the City University of New York, the most powerful causal influence on the religious lives of American teenagers and young adults is the religious lives of their parents. Parental influence while their children are living at home lasts after their departure for years, decades, and often lifetimes. Crucial to transmitting faith are a warm, affirming relationship between the parents and children, conversations in which the children ask questions and talk about religion in their lives, and the conveyance of consistency and meaning in the parents' religious teachings and related conduct.[214]

Smith and Adamczyk attribute the significance of parents to cultural shifts in our society. A while back many Americans took for granted that they belonged to a particular church or synagogue with the authority to teach the right way to live. But now we have more freedom to decide who we want to be and how we want to live, and we keep changing our views throughout our lives. Under these circumstances, families provide a place where we can talk about what matters to us and how to make good choices.[215]

As described by Smith and Adamczyk, parents still maintain their traditional role of passing down their faith. To do so, they are more effective if they exemplify it by their conduct, talk about what it means and why it matters, and combine clear expectations with emotional warmth. But simply passing down their faith is not enough in today's culture with its changing views of spirituality. Parents now have an additional role of teaching their children how to make decisions about their spiritual development in later years. By talking about good choices, parents help their children learn the skills needed in our society to keep reassessing their spiritual direction.[216]

Substituting for my parents, my grandparents passed along their faith so that I would take it to heart. During the disruptive stay with my mother and stepfather, a remnant of faith continued to shape me, and that was enough for me to rework my religious views in later years as a basic part of my identity. Some of my friends who grew up in religious homes had similar experiences. Even though their views or circumstances changed, they still had the wherewithal to keep searching for answers until they made sense of their spiritual concerns.

In the case of my friend Ben, he took his Jewish upbringing so seriously that he studied historical accounts of ancient Israel. At first, his research made him skeptical about whether the exodus really happened. This caused him so much anguish at Passover that he expressed his plight this way: "Can you imagine how I felt? There I was celebrating Passover with my children, and I knew it never even happened." Ben eventually found ways to reconcile a historical perspective with faith. He reasoned that the exodus really happened, but biblical writers exaggerated the event to emphasize divine power. To him, these embellishments made the story less believable, but the basic account was still compelling. Ben concluded that a historical approach ultimately strengthens faith because "you don't need to believe the unbelievable or defend the indefensible."

My friend Emily took a different approach. She had been living with her parents and siblings in an orderly churchgoing home when she was struck by polio. After that, her grandmother came over every day to help her parents and nurse her through recovery. From her grandmother's love and care, Emily distilled the basic principles that guided the rest of her life: We are called to love and serve each other, and through our love, God lives in us, and we live in God. For Emily, these spiritual connections had a powerful impact. When she had a major operation on her back due to complications of polio in later life, her friends supported her through the surgery by their prayers. For a few days afterward, she hovered unconscious between life and death. After she became fully conscious, she attributed her survival to their prayers: "I could have lived or died, and their prayers pushed me toward life."

My friend Karl had a less inspiring religious upbringing. When he was a young child, the teachers at his religious school warned children to watch out for the devil lurking behind every bush. He became so terrified of the devil that his parents sent him to a public school. Although his parents were regular churchgoers, they seldom talked about religion at home. Going to church was a conventional routine that was never discussed. Sunday school was no help either. When Karl questioned in class whether God existed, his teacher complained to the pastor, who discussed Karl's impropriety with his mother. Left on his own to answer his question, Karl could not find any rational proof of religious beliefs and dismissed involvement in any faith at all. Instead of internalizing the religious views of his family or church, he found the secular norms of his college professors and friends more in line with his intellectual views.

When people have faith, Karl attributed its roots to the culture in which they live. To persons of faith, he said, "It provides a sense of meaning, belonging, identity, and support." By contrast, he said, "The childhoods of others like me do not instill faith." Yet he was curious about how the Bible was written and how it reflected human aspirations, and he tried to live by ethical principles in his work and personal life. He concluded that even if we are not religious, we can view the Bible as an ancient text that encourages us to center our lives on our deepest values.

When Grandma talked to me before her surgery, she had a simple message to convey: Life is better when we put our trust in the Lord. For many people, the values instilled in us as children provide a framework for the rest of our lives. Like the scribes writing Deuteronomy, we may expand our views as our cultural perspectives and personal circumstances change. But we are still guided by core values that shape who we are and where we are going.

15

Choosing the Best Way

What has helped you choose a fulfilling way to live?

DEUTERONOMY 8:6–18 (WEALTH FROM THE LORD); 10:17–19 AND 24:17–22 (ORPHAN, WIDOW, AND NON-ISRAELITE RESIDENT); 15:1–11 (NEEDY NEIGHBOR); 30:1–20 (CHOOSE LIFE)

WHILE I STAYED AT my grandparents' farm, I would walk to the mailbox along the side of the country road to get our mail and then watch Grandma sit down at the kitchen table to go through it. Whenever she got a letter from Boys Town, she pointed it out to me. As soon as I saw the letter, I recognized its logo of a boy carrying his little brother on his back. Then Grandma put her contribution in an envelope and mailed it back to Boys Town.

Edward Flanagan, a Catholic priest, started Boys Town in Nebraska in 1917. He believed that each child could become a productive citizen if given love along with a home, education, and trade. Regardless of race, creed, or culture, he was interested in the neediest and most helpless children even if they had been in prison for serious crimes. Over the years, Boys Town expanded to more locations with a variety of services for boys and girls and their families.

Grandma's donations to Boys Town had a powerful influence on me. Ever since I became a lawyer, I planned to give at least half of my assets to organizations helping abused and neglected children, and in recent years, I learned that community foundations like the New York Community Trust are effective ways to leave legacies to such causes.

Grandma also influenced my adoption of a child in foster care. Given my familiarity with the ravages of parental abuse, I wanted to make the same difference for my daughter that my grandparents had made for me. In doing so, I learned how poorly foster children are treated by schools and social service agencies. Although foster children have many rights under the law, their rights are easily denied because they do not have parents who fight on their behalf. Given this disparity, I advocated for the welfare of disadvantaged youth at a number of government hearings.

Deuteronomy affirms the values that my grandparents passed down to me. It encourages us to appreciate everything we have been given and respond with gratitude and generosity. We need not worry that doing so leads to a dreary life of self-sacrifice. Reaching out to others is not a burden. It is the path to our own fulfillment.

THE BIBLE'S STORY

Near the end of Deuteronomy, the Israelites made a dramatic choice about how they wanted to live. By delivering them out of slavery to the promised land, God had given them the opportunity to have an abundant life, enjoying home, family, work, and community. But their enjoyment depended on reverence for God and obedience to his commands. Although at first glance the many laws in Deuteronomy may seem onerous, if we take a deeper look, we can appreciate how these laws would have guided the Israelites to a better life, and even if they fell short, they could still return to living God's way.

In Deuteronomy 8:6–18, Moses advised the Israelites to be humble about their success. God was giving them a land of wheat and barley, vines and fig trees, and pomegranates, olive oil, and honey, along with streams flowing past iron stones and copper hills. The Israelites should never forget that the Lord had given them everything they needed for a bountiful life. When they had eaten their fill and built fine houses, and when their herds and flocks and their silver and gold had multiplied, they should not exalt themselves, forgetting the Lord their God. Instead of taking credit for their good fortune, they should acknowledge their wealth came from the Lord: "Do not say to yourself, 'My power and the might of my own hand have gotten me this wealth.' But remember the LORD your God, for it is he who gives you power to get wealth."[217]

As presented in Deuteronomy, reaching out to the disadvantaged was one of the best ways to show gratitude for everything God had done. Of special concern were economically vulnerable orphans, widows, and non-Israelite residents who lived in the community without title to land. As told in Deuteronomy 10:17–19 and 24:17–22, the great, mighty, and awesome God of the Israelites showed no favor and took no bribes in the judicial system, but upheld the cause of orphans and widows, and loved non-Israelite residents, providing them with food and clothing. To imitate God, the Israelites should extend the same love and justice to a non-Israelite resident as they would to an Israelite; they should not deprive an orphan of justice or take a widow's garments to secure a loan; and they should leave food in their fields, olive groves, and vineyards for orphans, widows, and non-Israelite residents. In support of these norms, the Israelites were reminded that they themselves had been resident aliens in Egypt and redeemed from slavery.[218]

In Deuteronomy 15:1–11, taking care of poor and needy neighbors was another obligation. In ancient times, the poor received loans as a form of welfare, and when they were overwhelmed by debt, they could sell themselves into slavery. If neighbors needed help, Moses said the Israelites should not be hard-hearted or tightfisted toward them: "You should rather open your hand, willingly lending enough to meet the need."[219] Lenders could not charge interest on a loan to an Israelite, and they could not take as security for a loan anything needed for work or survival. To prevent poverty from lasting from one generation to the next, the Israelites were required to cancel the debts of fellow Israelites and release them from servitude every seven years.[220]

After covering social ethics along with other laws for the community, Moses elaborated on the statement in Deuteronomy 11:26–28 that he was setting forth a blessing if the Israelites obeyed the Lord's commandments and a curse if they turned away from these commands. In Deuteronomy 27:11—28:68, blessings included children, crops, and livestock, while curses included devastation and starvation. Although the blessings and curses usually were described as future possibilities, because of sins the Israelites already had committed, they would be cursed by foreign invaders like the Assyrians and Babylonians.[221]

Then the text takes a surprising turn. In Deuteronomy 30:1–5, Moses acknowledged that the Israelites would be driven in exile to Babylon due to their disobedience of God's laws. Yet the Lord would restore their fortunes and have compassion on them once they returned to him. Even if they had been exiled to the ends of the world, from there the Lord would gather them and bring them back. To reassure the exilic community, Moses used the Hebrew word *shuv*, which can mean "return," "repent," or "restore," to connect human repentance with divine forgiveness. This notion of returning developed into the rabbinic doctrine of repentance, which replaced the priestly idea of sacrificial atonement.[222]

As provided in Deuteronomy 30:6–10, to make obedience easier, God would open the heart of the Israelites so they would love the Lord with all their heart and soul. Circumcision had been a physical sign of belonging to the covenant between God and Israel; now it would be matched by an inward conversion. In a spiritual sense, God would cut away blockages between God and the heart of the Israelites to make their mind, will, and emotion come together with a single purpose. Consequently, the Israelites would keep the Lord's commandments, and the Lord would make the Israelites prosperous with many offspring and delight in their well-being.[223]

In Deuteronomy 30:11, Moses assured the Israelites that God's command was "not too hard for you, nor is it too far way." The command was not in heaven, so they need not ask who would go up there to get it for them. Nor was it beyond the sea, so they need not ask who would cross the waters to get it. Rather, by the customary educational method of reading, teaching, and reciting the text aloud, they would find that "the word is very near to you; it is in your mouth and in your heart for you to observe."[224]

A dramatic conclusion to the covenant requirements occurs in Deuteronomy 30:15–20. In Deuteronomy 30:15, Moses put before the Israelites the stark alternatives of "life and prosperity, death and adversity." As the Israelites entered the land, their future well-being would be entirely in their own hands. It would depend on the choice made by each person to live in obedience to the covenant. If they loved the Lord and walked in his ways, they would thrive and increase. Otherwise, they would perish. Moses urged them, "I have set before you life and death, blessings and curses. Choose life."[225]

This striking choice of life or death still invites reflection on the best way to live. In Jewish doctrine, the passage affirms the free will of individuals to choose between good and evil. In explaining the doctrine, the Jewish medieval scholar Maimonides refers to Genesis 3:22 in the garden of Eden story where the Lord acknowledged that humans have the capacity to know good and evil. To prove that free will is a fundamental concept of the Torah, Maimonides points to the choice of life or death in Deuteronomy 30:15, buttressed by the blessings and curses in Deuteronomy 11:26–28. He says these passages imply that the choice of good or evil is entirely up to each person.[226]

Even if we no longer envision all of Deuteronomy's blessings and curses, we know that our decisions will have serious consequences for ourselves and the people around us. If we live with gratitude and generosity, we will benefit our communities and find our own happiness.

WRITING THE STORY

Within the framework of an ancient Near Eastern treaty, the Israelite scribes inserted laws influenced by ancient Near Eastern legal codes, including long-standing concern for the disadvantaged. But these laws were ideals for the community's guidance rather than rigid requirements that would be strictly enforced. The Israelites' own experience of hardship and deliverance shaped their view of a merciful God who would forgive their lapses and restore their well-being.

The protection of orphans, widows, and the poor had been a policy of Mesopotamia and Egypt since early times.[227] By voicing concern for the weak, kings demonstrated their piety, justice, and legitimacy. As far back as 2400 BCE, a treaty between a god and Mesopotamian king specified that the mighty were not allowed to do injustice to orphans and widows.[228] During Hammurabi's rule over Babylon from 1792 to 1750 BCE, the prologue to his legal code said that the gods had called him to bring about the rule of righteousness and destroy the wicked so that the strong could not harm the weak, and the epilogue specifically protected orphans and widows.[229]

When the Israelite scribes included similar protections for the disadvantaged in Deuteronomy, they did so in a way that reflected their own understanding of God and royalty. Instead of saying a Mesopotamian king was great, mighty, and awesome, they attributed these qualities to their God. Instead of looking to a king to ensure justice in court and defend the disadvantaged, they praised their God for breaking into history to redeem the Israelite slaves and protect the marginalized. In response to these divine acts, the Israelites themselves were expected to reach out to the disadvantaged.[230]

The provisions in Deuteronomy for cancelling debt and freeing slaves illustrate another difference in its approach from other ancient Near Eastern cultures. To gain favor upon coming to the throne, ancient Near Eastern rulers sometimes cancelled debts owed to the monarchy and freed its indentured servants. In Deuteronomy, instead of a king, wealthy Israelites were expected to forgive the debts and unpaid labor contracts of the poor, and instead of a one-time event, better-off Israelites were supposed to take such actions every seven years.[231]

Deuteronomy itself indicates that its vision for the Israelite community was too utopian to be practical. Even though the text said no one would be poor if the Israelites lived as God intended, the text told them to give to the poor because someone would always be in need. When Jerusalem fell to the Babylonians, the Israelite prophet Jeremiah attributed the city's destruction to divine punishment because the Israelites had freed indentured slaves and afterward had immediately enslaved them. As Deuteronomy observed, Israel's breach of its covenant with God already was so severe that it would cause foreigners like the Assyrians and Babylonians to invade.[232]

After the Israelites were living in exile in Babylon, the passage in Deuteronomy 30:1–10 apparently was added to the text to give hope to the exiles. If they repented, the Lord would forgive them and spiritually cut away blockages in their hearts so that they would love the Lord with all their heart and soul. This passage reflected the views of the Israelite prophets who by then were saying that God would end the suffering of the Israelites and give them a new beginning. The prophet Ezekiel said God would replace their hearts of stone and give them a new heart and spirit so that they would obey divine laws. The prophet Jeremiah said that God would make a new covenant with the Israelites pursuant to which God would put the law within them and write it on their hearts.[233]

In Deuteronomy 30:11–14, the text returns to the covenant requirements presented by Moses. In the language of Near Eastern treaties, Moses commanded the Israelites to love the Lord and walk in his ways, which meant loyalty and obedience to God. Given Israel's understanding of the wisdom tradition, Moses assured his people that this command would not be too difficult for them. In the ancient Near East, divine wisdom was generally considered beyond human reach as if in the sky or under the earth. To the contrary, in Israel, the wisdom of God's laws had been revealed to everyone. It was not in the heavens or across the sea but rather in the hearts and recited in the mouths of the Israelites.[234]

The dramatic choice faced by the Israelites in Deuteronomy 30:15–20 was influenced by both ancient Near Eastern treaties and wisdom literature. Like Near Eastern treaties, the text contrasted blessings and curses exemplified by prosperity and adversity. Like wisdom instruction, the text contrasted life or death as the consequence of human choice. Moses integrated these alternatives by talking about "life and prosperity, death and adversity." Then he urged the Israelites to choose life so that they could live in the land given to their ancestors Abraham, Isaac, and Jacob.[235]

LIVING BY THE STORY

Like the Israelites, each of us faces a choice about the best way to live the rest of our lifetime. The entire book of Deuteronomy seems designed to help us make this decision. Even though the book drew on the culture of its time, it resonates with our concerns today. The text anticipated how the Israelites, like us, would take credit for their prosperity rather than respond in gratitude for all that had been given to them. The text also encouraged a concern for the poor and vulnerable that stretched back thousands of years. As a foster mother, I was intrigued to see that Deuteronomy not only considered food for orphans; it even anticipated bias against them in the judicial system. If we want a fair and just society, we need to uphold their cause in the courts.

Given the inspiration I found in Deuteronomy, I was surprised to hear my friend Elizabeth say how much the biblical laws troubled her. She was a lifelong Catholic, always involved in the church and helping the disadvantaged. To me, she modeled what the Bible tells us to do. But that was not the way she saw it. To her, the biblical laws made God seem rigid, demanding, and judgmental. She said that she did not have a positive view of the Ten Commandments and other laws in the Old Testament, and Jesus seemed to make things worse.

As Elizabeth knew, Jesus said that he came not to abolish but to fulfill the law. By this he meant the law in the Bible's first five books known to Jews as the Torah. His teachings sometimes proposed a deeper obedience to the law or an additional ethic for his followers. For example, he taught people to love not only their neighbors but also their enemies, and concluded by saying, "Be perfect, therefore, as your heavenly Father is perfect."[236]

Choosing the Best Way

Elizabeth was especially disturbed by the story Jesus told to illustrate what it means to love one another. When a young man asked what he needed to do for eternal life, Jesus told him to keep the commandments, named some of the Ten Commandments, and added loving your neighbor as yourself. After the young man said he already kept these laws, Jesus replied, "If you wish to be perfect, go, sell your possessions, and give the money to the poor, . . . then come, follow me."[237] Upon hearing this, the young man went away grieving, for he had many possessions.

As Elizabeth told me, when she heard what Jesus said about perfection, she thought to herself, "Whoa, that's a high bar. This guy is a tough taskmaster." For many years, she struggled with his demands until she finally saw him as compassionate rather than judgmental. She felt grateful that Jesus always had been a loving presence in her life, helping her treat others with greater kindness, and giving her more peace and joy. Feeling gratitude for all that he had done, she realized that he encourages us to be our best self, but never gives up on us when we lose our way, and his teachings are meant to inspire us, not to dictate strict compliance. Upon this realization, she felt she could follow in his footsteps as a loving guide to her deepest values.

Deuteronomy reinforces this perspective. It begins by reminding us of God's compassion, delivering the Israelites from slavery and giving them the promised land. In response, it encourages us to live with humility, generosity, justice, and compassion. The ending assures us of divine mercy when we fail to live up to our potential and need to turn around our lives.

When Deuteronomy offers the Israelites a choice of either life and prosperity or death and adversity, I do not see the alternatives as a promise of longevity and riches versus a judgment of destruction. We do not become vastly wealthy by living God's way, and we do not die if we violate divine teachings. I see the choice as more profound. When we use our spiritual, social, and economic resources to create satisfying lives for ourselves and our global community, we also find our own fulfillment.

Carrying on the Dream

What are your dreams for a better world?

BEFORE MY GRANDPARENTS' FARM was auctioned off to the highest bidder, I picked out Great-Grandpa's rocking chair to take back to New York. I remember him sitting in the chair while he watched the women scurrying around the kitchen to prepare food for the day. After Great-Grandpa died, Grandpa would sit there, and after his death, Uncle Bill. A few years later when his son-in-law Matt died, the farm was sold because no one was left to work the land. Now I rock back and forth in my Manhattan apartment with fond memories of the farm.

I am grateful that my relatives passed down to me the dream of a better world. As recounted in Deuteronomy 34, Moses shared this dream when he saw the promised land from a mountaintop right before he died. Martin Luther King Jr. felt the same way. The night before he was assassinated, he said that he, like Moses, might not reach the promised land, but we as a people would get there.

My favorite vision in the Bible is the coming of a better world so that all of us can live in God's image as intended at creation. The earth as God's kingdom is the prayer of Jews in the Kaddish and Christians in the Lord's Prayer, prayers that bring forth the hope of Jews for a messianic age of peace and of Christians for the second coming of Christ, the Messiah. While some Jews and Christians take these concepts literally, others see them as visions for a renewal of this world. Conservative Judaism expresses this hope by saying, "No human being can live without a dream."[238]

After I considered the Bible in light of its historical origins, I realized that my family on the farm gave me more than love. They also gave me hope. Their optimism was reinforced by biblical stories that acknowledge the ugly side of human nature while showing us how to live in God's image. We may identify with Abraham leaving the past behind for the promised land and the Israelite slaves saved from abuse to experience justice and freedom. Even people in our secular culture can appreciate the Bible's vision of a promised land where everyone can flourish. As long as we have this dream, we can make it through tough times and live with greater joy.

Endnotes

1. Gaustad and Schmidt, *Religious History of America*, 291; Kugel, *How to Read the Bible*, 2-5, 40-45. Beginning in the nineteenth century, the documentary hypothesis posited that the Bible's first five books were composed from four main strands: (1) J from the period of David and Solomon during the tenth century BCE, (2) E from the Northern Kingdom of Israel after Solomon's death, (3) D from the reforms of King Josiah of Judah in the late seventh century BCE, and (4) P for a priestly source during the Babylonian exile in the sixth century BCE. Now many scholars consider J and E to be a single, composite strand from a variety of sources. All the strands tend to be seen as trajectories developing over time. Marc Z. Brettler, "Introduction to the Pentateuch," in Coogan, *New Oxford Annotated Bible*, 3-6.

2. The Presbyterian Church (USA) provides this rationale for studying how the Bible was written: "The Scriptures, given under the guidance of the Holy Spirit, are nevertheless the words of men, conditioned by the language, thought forms, and literary fashions of the places and times at which they were written. They reflect views of life, history, and the cosmos which were then current. The church, therefore, has an obligation to approach the Scriptures with literary and historical understanding. As God has spoken his word in diverse cultural situations, the church is confident that he will continue to speak through the Scriptures in a changing world and in every form of human culture." "The Confession of 1967," in *Book of Confessions*, 285-97, para. 9.29.

3. For a discussion of this perspective, see Carr, *Holy Resilience*, 1-6.

4. See Carr, *Hebrew Bible*, 213-21, discussing the composition by the priests during the exile of the creation story making men and women in God's image. In scholarly works, material reflecting the views of priests is sometimes identified as "P," a "priestly source," or priests and persons associated with them. This book simply attributes such material to priests.

5. Genesis 1:3.

6. Genesis 1:26 as translated in Carr, *Hebrew Bible*, 219, using italics in the translation to emphasize connection between creation in God's image and rule over creation.

7. Genesis 1:27-28.

8. David M. Carr, "Genesis," in Coogan, *New Oxford Annotated Bible*, note on Genesis 1:26-27; Jon D. Levenson, "Genesis," in Berlin and Brettler, *Jewish Study Bible*, note

ENDNOTES

on Genesis 1:26–28.

9. Jon D. Levenson, "Genesis," in Berlin and Brettler, *Jewish Study Bible*, note on Genesis 1:26–28, citing Leviticus 25:23–24.

10. To avoid Christian references, BCE (before the common era) and CE (the common era) replace BC (before Christ) and AD (*anno domini*, in the year of the Lord).

11. Carr, *Introduction to the Old Testament*, 80–81; Hayes, *Introduction to the Bible*, 29–40; Matthews and Benjamin, *Old Testament Parallels*, 21–31 (dating and vignettes).

12. Carr, *Hebrew Bible*, 219, regarding Mesopotamian and Egyptian texts.

13. H. Smith, *World's Religions*, 281.

14. 2 Kings 25:7.

15. See Dorfner, "Grow Happiness"; Sparks, "Connecting Spirituality and Stress Relief."

16. Carr, *Introduction to the Old Testament*, 83.

17. Genesis 2:18. Instead of the phrase translated as "helper as his partner," a more literal translation would be a helper for the human that "corresponds to him," recognizing the need for companionship, even in the garden, to work. David M. Carr, "Genesis," in Coogan, *New Oxford Annotated Bible*, note on Genesis 2:18.

18. Genesis 2:23–24, quoting "bone of my bones" and "clings to his wife."

19. Gaustad and Schmidt, *Religious History of America*, 250.

20. Trible, *God and the Rhetoric*, 75–105.

21. Gowan, *From Eden to Babel*, 46.

22. See Carr, *Hebrew Bible*, 199–212, for the composition by the scribes in the Bible's first five books. These writers were non-priestly scribes sometimes referred to as "non-P," "non-priestly," or "a lay source" in scholarly works. For the creation and flood stories, these scribes are sometimes identified as "J," and for Deuteronomy, these scribes are sometimes identified as "D." For other parts of the Bible's first five books, these scribes are sometimes identified as "J," "E," or "JE." This book simply refers to them as scribes.

23. Hayes, *Introduction to the Bible*, 43–50 (dating and description of epic); Matthews and Benjamin, *Old Testament Parallels*, 38–43 (vignettes about Enkidu and the Wise Woman).

24. For a discussion of depictions of God, see Kugel, *Great Shift*, 59–71 (garden of Eden), 168–69 (Genesis 1 creation story), 169–76 (Hebrew Bible generally).

25. Christopher R. Matthews, "The Gospel According to Luke," in Attridge, *HarperCollins Study Bible*, note on Luke 23:43.

26. Jacobs, *Book of Jewish Belief*, 234.

27. Putnam and Campbell, *American Grace*, 490–92.

28. Putnam and Campbell, *American Grace*, 444–54.

29. Putnam and Campbell, *American Grace*, 471–79, 490–92.

30. Putnam and Campbell, *American Grace*, 478.

31. Marchese, "Yale's Happiness Professor," para 4.

32. Genesis 3:4–5.

33. Genesis 3:16; Carr, *Hebrew Bible*, 93–95.

34. Trible, *God and the Rhetoric*, 105–39.

35. Genesis 3:20.

36. See Hayes, *Introduction to the Bible*, 41–42, 48–50.

37. As suggested in David M. Carr, "Genesis," in Coogan, *New Oxford Annotated Bible*, note on Genesis 4:3–5, the ancient Israelite audience may have assumed a divine preference for animal sacrifices offered by Abel over the vegetable sacrifices offered by

Endnotes

Cain. Others note that Cain did not offer firstfruits comparable to Abel's firstborn as required by Old Testament passages such as Leviticus 23:9 (first fruit) and 27:26 (firstborn). In Hebrews 11:4, the New Testament suggests that Abel's faith made his offering more acceptable.

38. Genesis 4:7.
39. Ronald Hendel, "Genesis," in Attridge, *HarperCollins Study Bible*, note on Genesis 4:6–7.
40. Carr, *Writing on the Tablet*, 17, 31.
41. See Carr, *Hebrew Bible*, 92–97.
42. Hayes, *Introduction to the Bible*, 43–50; Matthews and Benjamin, *Old Testament Parallels*, 38–43 (vignettes about Enkidu and the Wise Woman).
43. In another example of wisdom's relationship to mortality in Mesopotamian literature, when the ruler of the divine assembly offered Adapa bread and water to make himself immortal, he refused the offer because his divine patron had created him to be wise but not immortal. See Carr, *Hebrew Bible*, 97 (Adam and Eve's mortality related to Near Eastern wisdom texts like Gilgamesh and Adapa epics); Hayes, *Introduction to the Bible*, 48–50 (Adam and Eve's mortality related to Gilgamesh epic); Matthews and Benjamin, *Old Testament Parallels*, 51–52 (vignette about Gilgamesh's mortality), 32–37 (vignette about Adapa's mortality).
44. Kugel, *How to Read the Bible*, 54–56 (transition from hunter-gatherer to agricultural society), 62–68 (origins of Cain's story); Carr, *Hebrew Bible*, 95–97.
45. Kugel, *How to Read the Bible*, xii.
46. Kugel, *How to Read the Bible*, 50–52 (Adam and Eve), 60–61 (Cain and Abel).
47. Kugel, *How to Read the Bible*, 341–42; Jon D. Levenson, "Genesis," in Berlin and Brettler, *Jewish Study Bible*, note on Genesis 3:22–24; Michael V. Fox, "Proverbs," in Berlin and Brettler, *Jewish Study Bible*, notes on Proverbs 3:17–18, 18.
48. Romans 5:12–21; 1 Corinthians 15:20–24, 42–49.
49. Paul Rigby, "Original Sin," in Fitzgerald, *Augustine through the Ages*, 607, 608.
50. Rotelle, *Sermons 148–83*, 43–44.
51. Cooper, "Medieval Jewish Version," 446–47, quoting the Talmud and describing its implications.
52. For the views of modern Christian theologians, see, e.g., Migliore, *Faith Seeking Understanding*, 158–63; Westermann, *Genesis*, 28–29.
53. Pinker, *Better Angels*, describes how violence has declined, including a discussion of killing family members (pp. 63–64), women's rights (pp. 394–415), and child abuse (pp. 415–47).
54. The priests' version of the creation and flood is set forth in Genesis 6:9–22; 7:6, 11, 13–16a, 18–21, 24; 8:1–2a, 3–5, 14–19; 9:1–19, 28–29. The scribes' version is found in the rest of Genesis 6:5—9:29. David M. Carr, "Genesis," in Coogan, *New Oxford Annotated Bible*, notes on Genesis 1:1—11:26; 9:18–29.
55. Genesis 8:21–22.
56. Genesis 6:9 (Noah's righteousness), 9:18–19 (Noah's sons populate earth); Ezekiel 14:14–20 (Noah so righteous he could save himself from annihilation).
57. Genesis 9:6.
58. For the relationship between the Bible and the Mesopotamian Atrahasis and Gilgamesh epics, see David M. Carr, "Genesis," in Coogan, *New Oxford Annotated Bible*, 9 (dating), notes on Genesis 6:5, 14–16; 8:4, 6–12, 20–22; Carr, *Hebrew Bible*, 90–91; Hayes, *Introduction to the Bible*, 52–55; Matthews and Benjamin, *Old Testament Parallels*,

ENDNOTES

46–51 (Utnapishtim story in Gilgamesh epic), 10–20 (flood story in Atrahasis epic).

59. Carr, *Introduction to the Old Testament*, 83.
60. For the scribes' narrative, see Carr, *Hebrew Bible*, 202–11.
61. For the priests' narrative, see Carr, *Hebrew Bible*, 213–21.
62. For Persian influence, see Carr, *Hebrew Bible*, 227–35.
63. Ezra 7:26.
64. For Ezra's reading of the Torah of Moses, see Nehemiah 8:1–3. For combining the scribes' and priests' narratives, see Carr, *Hebrew Bible*, 236–41.
65. David M. Carr, "Genesis," in Coogan, *New Oxford Annotated Bible*, note on Genesis 6:5—8:19.
66. H. Smith, *World's Religions*, 292.
67. White, *Great Big Book*, 161, 172, 344, 400.
68. Pinker, *Better Angels*, 195–96.
69. Joshua 24:2.
70. David M. Carr, "Genesis," in Coogan, *New Oxford Annotated Bible*, notes on Genesis 12:2.
71. Jon D. Levenson, "Genesis," in Berlin and Brettler, *Jewish Study Bible*, note on Genesis 15:6.
72. David M. Carr, "Genesis," in Coogan, *New Oxford Annotated Bible*, notes on Genesis 16:1–16, 4–5.
73. Genesis 16:11, note v, for Ishmael; and 16:13, note w, for El-roi.
74. David M. Carr, "Genesis," in Coogan, *New Oxford Annotated Bible*, notes on Genesis 17:5, 15.
75. See David M. Carr, "Genesis," in Coogan, *New Oxford Annotated Bible*, note on Genesis 18:2–8; Jon D. Levenson, "Genesis," in Berlin and Brettler, *Jewish Study Bible*, note on Genesis 18:1–2.
76. For Isaac's name, see Genesis 17:19, note d; 21:3; David M. Carr, "Genesis," in Coogan, *New Oxford Annotated Bible*, note on Genesis 18:12.
77. David M. Carr, "Genesis," in *New Oxford Annotated Bible*, note on Genesis 21:9 ("playing" translated literally would be "making [him] laugh").
78. Jon D. Levenson, "Genesis," in Berlin and Brettler, *Jewish Study Bible*, note on Genesis 25:1.
79. For composition of the Abraham stories, see David M. Carr, "Genesis," in Coogan, *New Oxford Annotated Bible*, 7–8 (overview), note on Genesis 11:27—25:11 (Abraham stories); Carr, *Hebrew Bible*, 202–5, 213–19, 222–24 (during exile, God's promise to Abraham written by scribes and covenant of circumcision written by priests); Kugel, *How to Read the Bible*, 103 (early versions of stories dating to tenth or eleventh century BCE or even earlier).
80. For the characteristics of the God of Old, see Kugel, *How to Read the Bible*, 107–18.
81. Compare Genesis 12:1–3 (God's call to Abraham) with Psalm 72:17 (praise of Israelite king), as discussed in Carr, *Hebrew Bible*, 222–24. For the tendency of exilic communities to focus on family traditions and regard ancient ancestors like royalty, see Carr, *Introduction to the Old Testament*, 171–72, 191–92, 203–5.
82. For emphasis on promise in stories about Abraham and his descendants, see Carr, *Hebrew Bible*, 203–5, 222–24.
83. For prophetic messages linked to Abraham, see Ezekiel 33:24; Isaiah 41:8; 51:2. For Abraham stories reinforcing prophetic message, see Carr, *Hebrew Bible*, 203–5,

Endnotes

222–24.

84. David M. Carr, "Genesis," in Coogan, *New Oxford Annotated Bible*, notes on Genesis 11:27—25:11; 16:1–16; 25:12–18, 16, 18 (origins of Ishmaelites, seen as ancestors of Arab peoples, placed in desert on either side of the Red Sea).

85. Jacobs, *Book of Jewish Belief*, 159–60.

86. Compare Genesis 15:6 with Romans 4; Galatians 3:6–9; Hebrews 11:8–12.

87. Dawood, Koran 3:66–72.

88. Sanadiki, *Legends & Narratives*, 95–98, 103–4.

89. Trible, *Texts of Terror*, 28–29; Williams, *Sisters in the Wilderness*, 6.

90. Amar, "End of Roe v. Wade," para. 16.

91. David M. Carr, "Genesis," in Coogan, *New Oxford Annotated Bible*, note on Genesis 22:1a.

92. Genesis 22:1–2.

93. Genesis 22:8.

94. Genesis 22:14.

95. Levenson, *Death and Resurrection*.

96. Levenson, *Death and Resurrection*, 8–9, 15–17. Exodus 22:29–30 is numbered Exodus 22:28–29 in Levenson's translation.

97. Levenson, *Death and Resurrection*, 11–12, 20–22, 36–37.

98. Levenson, *Death and Resurrection*, 4–5, 43–45, citing Jeremiah 19:5–6; Ezekiel 20:25–26; Deuteronomy 12:31; Leviticus 18:21, 20:2–5.

99. Carr, *Hebrew Bible*, 205.

100. See David M. Carr, "Genesis," in Coogan, *New Oxford Annotated Bible*, note on Genesis 22:1b–2 (story is not polemic against child sacrifice; it assumes child sacrifice could be performed under extraordinary circumstances); Jon D. Levenson, "Genesis," in Berlin and Brettler, *Jewish Study Bible*, note on Genesis 22:13 (the story is not a polemic against child sacrifice; it rewards Abraham for being willing to carry out Lord's command).

101. Feld, *Mahzor Lev Shalem*, 103, citing Abraham protesting the destruction of Sodom and Gomorrah in Genesis 18.

102. John 3:16.

103. Hebrews 11:17–19.

104. See, e.g., Brueggemann, *Genesis*, 185–94.

105. Dawood, Koran 37:91–105.

106. Sanadiki, *Legends & Narratives*, 99. In the Bible, Genesis 22:2 locates Isaac's near sacrifice on a mountain in "the land of Moriah," and 2 Chronicles 3:1 locates the Jerusalem temple on Mount Moriah.

107. See "The Sacrifice of Isaac: A Survivor's Story," in Wiesel, *Messengers of God*, 69–97.

108. David M. Carr, "Genesis," in *New Oxford Annotated Bible*, notes on Genesis 25:25, 26.

109. Genesis 25:34. See David M. Carr, "Genesis," in Coogan, *New Oxford Annotated Bible*, note on Genesis 25:31–34 for meaning of birthright and for Israel's relationship to Edom explaining Esau's unflattering portrayal.

110. See David M. Carr, "Genesis," in Coogan, *New Oxford Annotated Bible*, notes on Genesis 27:4, 34–35 on blessing.

111. Genesis 32:28.

112. Genesis 32:30.

Endnotes

113. Genesis 33:9–10.
114. For a description of village life, see Carr, *Hebrew Bible*, 36–38.
115. For trickster tradition and Jacob stories, see Carr, *Hebrew Bible*, 49–51.
116. Carr, *Hebrew Bible*, 104.
117. See Carr, *Hebrew Bible*, 52, 205–6; David M. Carr, "Genesis," in Coogan, *New Oxford Annotated Bible*, notes on Genesis 28:12, 13–15 (promise at Bethel).
118. Benedict XVI, *Verbum Domini*, 75–76.
119. Benedict XVI, "General Audience," paras. 6 ("true identity as a deceiver" and "new name as a sign of a new identity"), 8 ("a long night of seeking God"), 10 ("gratuitous gift that ultimately allows us to recognize the Lord's face").
120. Carr, *Hebrew Bible*, 105; Carr, "Genesis," in Coogan, *New Oxford Annotated Bible*, notes on Genesis 37:1—50:26; 44:18–34.
121. Kugel, *How to Read the Bible*, 181–83, 184–85.
122. Kugel, *How to Read the Bible*, 183–84; Stephen A. Geller, "The Religion of the Bible," in Berlin and Brettler, *Jewish Study Bible*, 1994–96 (wisdom tradition).
123. Kugel, *Great Shift*, 22–30, 33–36.
124. Brueggemann, *Genesis*, 292–96, 316–20, 343–50.
125. National Scientific Council on the Developing Child, *Supportive Relationships and Active Skill-Building*, 1.
126. Carol Meyers, "Exodus," in Coogan, *New Oxford Annotated Bible*, 83; Jeffrey H. Tigay, "Exodus," in Berlin and Brettler, *Jewish Study Bible*, 98–99.
127. Childs, *Book of Exodus*, 212–14, 237–39.
128. Carol Meyers, "Exodus," in Coogan, *New Oxford Annotated Bible*, notes on Exodus 2:15b, 3:1.
129. Exodus 3:4.
130. Jeffrey H. Tigay, "Exodus," in Berlin and Bressler, *Jewish Study Bible*, note on Exodus 3:8 (milk and honey as vision of fertile land).
131. Exodus 3:12.
132. Exodus 3:14–15.
133. Carol Meyers, "Exodus," in Coogan, *New Oxford Annotated Bible*, notes on Exodus 3:14, 15; Jeffrey H. Tigay, "Exodus," in Berlin and Bressler, *Jewish Study Bible*, note on Exodus 3:14–15.
134. Carol Meyers, "Exodus," in Coogan, *New Oxford Annotated Bible*, note on Exodus 12:37; Jeffrey H. Tigay, "Exodus," in Berlin and Brettler, *Jewish Study Bible*, note on Exodus 12:37.
135. The historicity of the exodus and the development of the exodus story as described in this section of this book rely on Michael D. Coogan, "Cultural Contexts," in Coogan, *New Oxford Annotated Bible*, 2292–93; Carol Meyers, "Exodus," in Coogan, *New Oxford Annotated Bible*, 81–82; Jeffrey H. Tigay, "Exodus," in Berlin and Brettler, *Jewish Study Bible*, 96–98.
136. Carol Meyers, "Exodus," in Coogan, *New Oxford Annotated Bible*, 82.
137. Carol Meyers, "Exodus," in Coogan, *New Oxford Annotated Bible*, note on Exodus 2:10; Jeffrey H. Tigay, "Exodus," in Berlin and Brettler, *Jewish Study Bible*, note on Exodus 2:10.
138. McAdams, *Redemptive Self*, 9, 85.
139. Norton, *To 1877*, 414.
140. McAdams, *Redemptive Self*.
141. McAdams, *Redemptive Self*, xiv, 24–25.

Endnotes

142. McAdams, *Redemptive Self*, 12–18, 26–27.
143. McAdams, *Redemptive Self*, xiii, 31–39, 134–39.
144. McAdams, *Redemptive Self*, 210–36.
145. Attributed to a priestly source, Exodus 6:3 says God's name was unknown to Abraham, Isaac, and Jacob. According to other sources, Genesis 4:26 says God's name was invoked at the time of Adam and Eve's grandchild, and Genesis 13:4 says Abraham called on God's name.
146. Exodus 6:6–7.
147. Carol Meyer, "Exodus," in Coogan, *New Oxford Annotated Bible*, note on Exodus 11:1—13:16.
148. Exodus 14:14, inserting "Yahweh" in place of the usual translation "Lord."
149. Exodus 15:3, inserting "Yahweh" in place of the usual translation "Lord."
150. See Carol Meyers, "Exodus," in Coogan, *New Oxford Annotated Bible*, notes on Exodus 2:15b (Midianites based in northwest Arabia led caravans across Sinai to Egypt) and 3:15 (temple inscription of Yahweh's name linked to desert-dwellers including Midianites). See also Kugel, *How to Read the Bible*, 424–28, referring to temple inscription and citing Deuteronomy 33:2 (Sinai, Seir, and Mount Paran); Judges 5:4–5 (Seir, Edom, and Sinai); Habakkuk 3:3 (Teman and Mount Paran); Psalm 68:7–8, which is Psalm 68:8–9 in Kugel's translation (Sinai). Sinai is believed to be south and east of ancient Israel, Mount Paran is south of Israel and west of Edom, Seir is a mountain in Edom, and Teman is a synonym for Edom.
151. Kugel, *How to Read the Bible*, 414–15, citing Exodus 15:3–6; Deuteronomy 33:26; Judges 5:4, 20, 23; Habakkuk 3:11–13; Psalm 68:7–8, which is Psalm 68:8–9 in Kugel's translation.
152. Carol Meyers, "Exodus," in Coogan, *New Oxford Annotated Bible*, note on Exodus 15:1–21 (dating of Song of the Sea); Kugel, *How to Read the Bible*, 228–231 (later narrative version of sea crossing).
153. Carol Meyers, "Exodus," in Coogan, *New Oxford Annotated Bible*, notes on Exodus 14:14; 15:1–21, 3. For comparison of El with Baal, see Hayes, *Introduction to the Bible*, 105–10, 116–18; Kugel, *How to Read the Bible*, 422–24.
154. Carr, *Hebrew Bible*, 207–8; Carr, *Holy Resilience*, 110–16.
155. Carr, *Holy Resilience*, 117–20; Kugel, *How to Read the Bible*, 322–25.
156. Jeffrey H. Tigay, "Exodus," in Berlin and Brettler, *Jewish Study Bible*, note on Exodus 14:20.
157. Lawson, *Understanding the Borderline Mother*, 121–49, 271–90.
158. Herman, *Trauma and Recovery*, 168–72.
159. Herman, *Trauma and Recovery*, 189–90.
160. Black, *Lord's Prayer*, 186–91.
161. Jeffrey H. Tigay, "Exodus," in Berlin and Brettler, *Jewish Study Bible*, note on Exodus 19:4.
162. Carol Meyers, "Exodus," in Coogan, *New Oxford Annotated Bible*, note on Exodus 19:6; Jeffrey H. Tigay, "Exodus," in Berlin and Brettler, *Jewish Study Bible*, note on Exodus 19:5b–6a.
163. Jewish tradition designates the opening statement as a commandment and combines into a single commandment the first and second ones above. For Catholics and Lutherans, the opening statement combines with the first and second commands above to form a single commandment, and the last command above is divided into two. Carol Meyers, "Exodus," in Coogan, *New Oxford Annotated Bible*, note on Exodus 20:1–17.

ENDNOTES

164. Jeffrey H. Tigay, "Exodus," in Berlin and Brettler, *Jewish Study Bible*, note on Exodus 20:1–14.

165. For the settlement of hilltop villages and the emergence of Israel on these hilltops, see Kugel, *How to Read the Bible*, 383–85.

166. For a description of village life, see Carr, *Hebrew Bible*, 36–38.

167. See Judges 5:15–17 (refusal of call to arms); Judges 19 (gang rape and death); 1 Samuel 8:10–18 (king's demand for taxes and labor).

168. For the relationship of Yahweh to tribal life, see Kugel, *How to Read the Bible*, 413–16.

169. Deuteronomy 33:5 as translated in Kugel, *How to Read the Bible*, 414. See also Bernard M. Levinson, "Deuteronomy," in Berlin and Brettler, *Jewish Study Bible*, notes on Deuteronomy 32:15 (*Jeshuran* referring to Israel); 33:5 (God as divine king).

170. For the relationship of covenant to a treaty with a foreign king, see Kugel, *How to Read the Bible*, 240–49, 413–16.

171. For the Ten Commandments as ethical standards of the tribal period, see Kugel, *How to Read the Bible*, 248–49, 413–16. For the Ten Commandments as teaching material, see Carr, *Hebrew Bible*, 150.

172. Carr, *Hebrew Bible*, 87–88, 98; Kugel, *How to Read the Bible*, 270–73. Kugel suggests that the Ten Commandments developed during Israel's first emergence as a nation, they were later conceived as a stipulation of a covenant, and still later they were supplemented by the Covenant Code. Kugel, *How to Read the Bible*, 247–49.

173. Herman, *Trauma and Recovery*, 155–213.

174. For more personal stories of recovering alcoholics, see McAdams, *Redemptive Self*, 198–202.

175. Jeffrey Stackert, "Leviticus," in Coogan, *New Oxford Annotated Bible*, 144–45, note on Leviticus 11:1—16:34.

176. Baruch J. Schwartz, "Leviticus," in Berlin and Brettler, *Jewish Study Bible*, notes on Leviticus 1:1—3:17 (voluntary sacrifices); 4:1—5:26 (sacrifices atoning for wrongs).

177. Baruch J. Schwartz, "Leviticus," in Berlin and Brettler, *Jewish Study Bible*, note on Leviticus 16:22.

178. Baruch J. Schwartz, "Leviticus," in Berlin and Brettler, *Jewish Study Bible*, notes on Leviticus 16:1–34, 29; 23:26–32.

179. Baruch J. Schwartz, "Leviticus," in Berlin and Brettler, *Jewish Study Bible*, note on Leviticus 26:40–42.

180. Baruch J. Schwartz, "Leviticus," in Berlin and Brettler, *Jewish Study Bible*, 195; Jeffrey Stackert, "Leviticus," in Coogan, *New Oxford Annotated Bible*, 143.

181. Kugel, *How to Read the Bible*, 284–89.

182. Kugel, *How to Read the Bible*, 325–26.

183. Jeffrey Stackert, "Leviticus," in Coogan, *New Oxford Annotated Bible*, notes on Leviticus 16:29–34a; 23:26–32 (holiness school additions). For a comparison of the holiness school with traditional priests and non-priestly writing, see Schwartz, "Leviticus," in Berlin and Brettler, *Jewish Study Bible*, notes on Leviticus 17–26; 19:1–37.

184. Jeffrey Stackert, "Leviticus," in Coogan, *New Oxford Annotated Bible*, notes on Leviticus 26:3–46, 33–45, 40–45 (holiness school addressing exile).

185. Feld, *Mahzor Lev Shalem*, 282.

186. Feld, *Mahzor Lev Shalem*, 40, 280.

187. Romans 3:25 (sacrifice of atonement), 5:9 (justified by his blood).

188. Philippians 4:7. See Carolyn Osiek, "The Letter of Paul to the Philippians," in

Endnotes

Coogan, *New Oxford Annotated Bible*, 2099-100, for Paul's circumstances.

189. Carr, *Introduction to the Old Testament*, 197, 199.

190. Thomas B. Dozeman, "Numbers," in Coogan, *New Oxford Annotated Bible*, 187.

191. Thomas B. Dozeman, "Numbers," in Coogan, *New Oxford Annotated Bible*, notes on Numbers 6:24-26, 27.

192. Numbers 20:1-13; 27:12-23 and Deuteronomy 32:48-52 suggest that Moses and Aaron did not enter the promised land because they had sinned by not following God's instructions for bringing water out of a rock. By contrast, Deuteronomy 1:37; 3:23-29; 4:21 suggest that Moses did not enter the promised land because he bore the sins of the Israelites.

193. Numbers 13:33.

194. Carr, *Hebrew Bible*, 216-19; Nili S. Fox, "Numbers," in Berlin and Brettler, *Jewish Study Bible*, 268.

195. See Thomas B. Dozeman, "Numbers," in Coogan, *New Oxford Annotated Bible*, 189; Kugel, *How to Read the Bible*, 313-14.

196. Stackert, "Leviticus," in Coogan, *New Oxford Annotated Bible*, note on Leviticus 20:26 (holy means "separated" for God). See Carr, *Holy Resilience*, 24-80 (biblical texts attributing Assyrian and Babylonian dominance to the sins of the Israelites), 121-24 (concerns about holiness and purity during the Babylonian exile).

197. Carr, *Holy Resilience*, 68-69, 129-32.

198. Thomas B. Dozeman, "Numbers," in Coogan, *New Oxford Annotated Bible*, 187-89, notes on Numbers 5:1—6:27; 6:22-27.

199. Carr, *Hebrew Bible*, 218, 239; Carr, *Holy Resilience*, 116, 124-27. Carr, *Hebrew Bible*, 215, lists priestly material in the spy mission in Numbers 13:1-17a, 21, 25-26, 32-33; 14:1-3, 5-10, 26-38.

200. Erikson, *Childhood and Society*, 247-69; Erikson, *Insight and Responsibility*, 115-18. For a discussion of Erikson's model, see McAdams, *Redemptive Self*, 31-35.

201. Bernard M. Levinson, "Deuteronomy," in Berlin and Brettler, *Jewish Study Bible*, notes on Deuteronomy 4:9; 5:3; 29:9, 10, 11, 13-14. Levinson also wrote commentary for "Deuteronomy," in Coogan, *New Oxford Annotated Bible*.

202. Matthew 22:34-40; Mark 12:28-31; Luke 10:25-28.

203. Carr, *Hebrew Bible*, 160-62.

204. Kugel, *How to Read the Bible*, 369, 431-32 (monotheism in Deuteronomy); Bernard M. Levinson, "Deuteronomy," in Berlin and Brettler, *Jewish Study Bible*, 342-43 (transition from monolatry to monotheism), notes on Deuteronomy 4:35 (monotheism); 5:7 (Ten Commandments); 6:4-9 (Shema).

205. Ziony Zevit, "2 Kings," in Berlin and Brettler, *Jewish Study Bible*, note on 2 Kings 22:3.

206. Carr, *Hebrew Bible*, 113-21; Carr, *Holy Resilience*, 26-37. In these texts, Carr addresses the concerns of modern readers with Hosea's portrayal of an unfaithful wife.

207. Carr, *Hebrew Bible*, 140-45.

208. For Deuteronomy's adaptation of a vassal treaty, see Carr, *Hebrew Bible*, 146-49; and Kugel, *How to Read the Bible*, 348-50, 353-55.

209. Bernard M. Levinson, "Deuteronomy," in Berlin and Brettler, *Jewish Study Bible*, notes on Deuteronomy 5:10; 6:5, 14.

210. Carr, *Hebrew Bible*, 149, 160-62; Bernard M. Levinson, "Deuteronomy," in Cogan, *New Oxford Annotated Bible*, note on Deuteronomy 6:4-5 ("Hear, O Israel").

211. Isaiah 43:10-13; 44:6-8; 45:6-7, 22. Carr, *Hebrew Bible*, 192; Benjamin D.

Endnotes

Sommer, "Isaiah," in Berlin and Brettler, *Jewish Study Bible*, 765–66.

212. Bernard M. Levinson, "Deuteronomy," in Berlin and Brettler, *Jewish Study Bible*, 342–43, notes on Deuteronomy 4:35; 5:7; 6:4–9.

213. For a discussion of how Deuteronomy balances tradition with the needs of contemporary generations, see Bernard M. Levinson, "Deuteronomy," in Berlin and Brettler, *Jewish Study Bible*, 339.

214. C. Smith and Adamczyk, *Handing Down the Faith*, 1–6.

215. C. Smith and Adamczyk, *Handing Down the Faith*, 73–88.

216. C. Smith and Adamczyk, *Handing Down the Faith*, 88–91 (developing self-direction), 224–26 (transmitting faith).

217. Deuteronomy 8:17–18.

218. Bernard M. Levinson, "Deuteronomy," in Berlin and Brettler, *Jewish Study Bible*, notes on 1:16 (same justice for Israelites and non-Israelite residents); 10:17–18 (social ethics of justice in court and defending marginalized based on imitating God); 10:18–19 (God's assurance of justice and protection of orphans, widows, and non-Israelite residents); 24:17 (upholding rights and leaving food for orphans, widows, and non-Israelite residents). Although the Hebrew term for non-Israelite resident is sometimes translated "resident alien" or "stranger," the note on Genesis 1:16 explains that the term refers to non-Israelite residents who live in the community without title to land and therefore are economically vulnerable.

219. Deuteronomy 15:8.

220. Deuteronomy 15:1–18 (canceling debts and releasing slaves); 23:19–20 (no interest on loans to Israelites); 24:6 (no loans secured by items needed for survival). Apparently due to the difficulty of enforcement, Leviticus 25:10, 39–44 extends the period for releasing indentured slaves from seven to fifty years.

221. Bernard M. Levinson, "Deuteronomy," in Berlin and Brettler, *Jewish Study Bible*, notes on Deuteronomy 28:47–57, 47, 48, 49–57, 52, 53–57.

222. Bernard M. Levinson, "Deuteronomy," in Berlin and Brettler, *Jewish Study Bible*, note on Deuteronomy 30:1–10, including Jewish doctrine of repentance.

223. Bernard M. Levinson, "Deuteronomy," in Berlin and Brettler, *Jewish Study Bible*, notes on Deuteronomy 10:16; 30:6.

224. Deuteronomy 30:14. Bernard M. Levinson, "Deuteronomy," in Berlin and Brettler, *Jewish Study Bible*, note on Deuteronomy 30:14.

225. Deuteronomy 30:19.

226. Bernard M. Levinson, "Deuteronomy," in Berlin and Brettler, *Jewish Study Bible*, note on Deuteronomy 30:15–20, citing Maimonides, *Hilkhot Teshuvah*, 5.3.

227. F. Charles Fensham, "Widow, Orphan, and the Poor in Ancient Near Eastern Legal and Wisdom Literature," in Greenspahn, *Essential Papers on Israel*, 176–92.

228. F. Charles Fensham, "Widow, Orphan, and the Poor in Ancient Near Eastern Legal and Wisdom Literature," in Greenspahn, *Essential Papers on Israel*, 177.

229. King, "Code of Hammurabi," paras. 1 and 3 of prologue and 1 of epilogue.

230. Bernard M. Levinson, "Deuteronomy," in Berlin and Brettler, *Jewish Study Bible*, note on Deuteronomy 10:17–18 (God rather than monarch providing for justice and disadvantaged, giving God royal attributes of great, mighty, and awesome).

231. Bernard M. Levinson, "Deuteronomy," in Berlin and Brettler, *Jewish Study Bible*, note on Deuteronomy 15:1–18.

232. Bernard M. Levinson, "Deuteronomy," in Berlin and Brettler, *Jewish Study Bible*, notes on Deuteronomy 15:4 (contrasting verses 4 and 7 on giving to the poor); 15:12–18

ENDNOTES

(release of slaves with reference to Jeremiah 34:6–22); 28:47 (future curse based on past wrongdoing).

233. Bernard M. Levinson, "Deuteronomy," in Berlin and Brettler, *Jewish Study Bible*, notes on Deuteronomy 30:1–10, 5, 6, citing Isaiah 42:9; 43:6–20; 51:9–11; Ezekiel 11:19–20; 36:26–27; Jeremiah 31:31–34.

234. Bernard M. Levinson, "Deuteronomy," in Berlin and Brettler, *Jewish Study Bible*, note on Deuteronomy 30:11–14.

235. Bernard M. Levinson, "Deuteronomy," in Berlin and Brettler, *Jewish Study Bible*, notes on Deuteronomy 30:16, 19.

236. Matthew 5:48. See J. R. C. Cousland, "The Gospel According to Matthew," in Coogan, *New Oxford Annotated Bible*, notes on Matthew 5:17–20, 21–48, 48.

237. Matthew 19:21.

238. For the position of Conservative Judaism, see "Eschatology: Our Vision of the Future," in The Jewish Theological Seminary of America et al., *Emet ve-Emunah*, 28–32 (quotation on p. 29).

Acknowledgments

I AM GRATEFUL TO my extended family for showing me how to integrate faith with our personal lives and for encouraging me while I wrote this book. I am also grateful for my Christian, Jewish, and secular friends who joined me for five years in a monthly discussion group. The people described in this book include some of my relatives and discussion group members.

At Union Theological Seminary in New York City, I benefitted from the advice and knowledge of several outstanding professors of the Hebrew Bible. David Carr, a specialist in how the Bible was written, was helpful from the time I first told him about my idea for this book through its many reiterations until publication. Since I have always admired Phyllis Trible as a groundbreaking biblical scholar, I was honored to get to know her and thrilled that she liked this book. As Esther Hamori was working on her own book, *God's Monsters*, she was supportive of mine.

While writing this book, I appreciated the opportunity to present material from the book to Terry Nelson's book group in Minneapolis and Craig Townsend's adult education class at St. Ann & the Holy Trinity Church in New York City. Julia Roller helped me develop the book, commented on the manuscript, and suggested ways to make the writing engaging. Abby Kendrick contributed ideas for marketing the book. I also benefitted from comments from several writing groups.

I am fortunate to have Wipf and Stock under its Cascade Books imprint as my publisher and K. C. Hanson as my editor. He brings to bear his teaching, writing, and editing experience as a biblical scholar. I was greatly honored that Walter Brueggemann, an esteemed professor of the Hebrew

Acknowledgments

Bible, endorsed the book. I also value the endorsements from other distinguished professors, clergy, and religiously involved people.

I want to thank all my friends who commented on drafts of the book. Jan Schwarz read the first draft of a couple chapters and many later drafts, George Shockey read the manuscript with special interest in its philosophical and historical aspects, and Lynne Malina read the manuscript with particular attention to its literary and psychological aspects. Other people who made valuable contributions include Micah Bloomfield, Ann Dille Bushe, Susan Buckley, Shawn Donovan, Alex Marano, Marillyn Mehr, and Henry and Lillian Parr.

Appendix A

Time Line of Israel's History and the Bible's First Five Books

THIS TIME LINE GIVES dates for major events affecting Israel and the Bible's first five books. The time line for historical events is generally based on the time line and chronology of rulers in Coogan, *New Oxford Annotated Bible*, 2308–15. The time line for development of the Bible's first five books is generally based on Carr, *Hebrew Bible*, xx–xxiii.

3000 BCE: EGYPT AND MESOPOTAMIA

By 3000 BCE, the great valleys of the Nile River in Egypt and the Tigris and Euphrates Rivers in Mesopotamia (now largely Iraq) had been urbanized, and writing had been invented.

2000 BCE: BIBLICAL ANCESTORS IN CANAAN

For many years after 3000 BCE, the area of the Middle East known as Canaan was often dominated by Egypt and Mesopotamia. The Bible places Abraham and Sarah and their progeny in this area during the early second millennium BCE, but they have not been documented by historical evidence outside of the Bible.

Appendix A

1279–1213 BCE: EXODUS FROM EGYPT

The exodus from Egypt portrayed in the Bible may have occurred during the reign of Pharaoh Rameses II from 1279 to 1213 BCE or his son Merneptah from 1213 to 1203 BCE. In the first mention of Israel outside of the Bible, a granite slab extolled Merneptah's military success in Canaan, including his victory over a group identified as "Israel."

1250–1005 BCE: HILL COUNTRY VILLAGES

From 1250 to 1005 BCE, many villages were established in the hill country of northern Israel, and tribal Israel emerged under Saul's chieftainship from 1025 to 1005 BCE. Around this time, the villagers may have told oral stories about biblical ancestors and the exodus.

1005–928 BCE: DAVID AND SOLOMON'S MONARCHY

Israel established a monarchy headed by David from 1005 to 965 BCE and by Solomon from 968 to 928 BCE, with Jerusalem as the capital. Royal scribes introduced writing and may have developed early versions of the creation and flood stories in Genesis and the Covenant Code in Exodus.

928 BCE: DIVIDED KINGDOM

In 928 BCE, Israel divided into a Northern Kingdom of Israel, eventually ruled from Samaria, and a Southern Kingdom of Judah, ruled from Jerusalem. The Northern Kingdom may have begun to write down oral stories about Jacob, Joseph, and the exodus.

722 BCE: FALL OF NORTHERN KINGDOM

In 722 BCE, the Assyrians conquered Samaria in the Northern Kingdom and dispersed its population. For many years, the Southern Kingdom was threatened by the Assyrians.

TIME LINE OF ISRAEL'S HISTORY AND THE BIBLE'S FIRST FIVE BOOKS

623 BCE: KING JOSIAH'S REFORMS

As Assyrian power waned, beginning in 623 BCE, King Josiah of Judah implemented religious reforms and sought control over the northern area. An early version of the book of Deuteronomy found in Jerusalem's temple during his reign supported his reforms. The text may have been taken from the Northern Kingdom to the Southern Kingdom after the Assyrian conquest.

586 BCE (OR 587 BCE BY SOME AUTHORITIES): FALL OF JERUSALEM

Around 586 BCE, the Babylonians captured Jerusalem and destroyed its temple. In several waves, the elite were exiled to Babylon. During the exile, scribes put together a sweeping account, including stories of the creation and the flood, biblical ancestors, the exodus, and Deuteronomy; and the priests wrote an alternative narrative emphasizing their concerns. The first datable reference to monotheism in the Bible occurs around this time.

538 BCE: RETURN TO JERUSALEM

After the Persian king Cyrus the Great conquered Babylon, some exiles began returning to Jerusalem in 538 BCE and later rebuilt the temple. The narratives of the scribes and priests were eventually combined into the Bible's first five books, known as the Torah to Jews and the Pentateuch to Christians.

515 BCE: COMPLETION OF SECOND TEMPLE

The temple was rebuilt in Jerusalem, beginning the era of temple-centered Judaism.

336–323 BCE: ALEXANDER THE GREAT

Alexander the Great conquered much of the known world, resulting in Greek domination of Israel.

Appendix A

142–63 BCE: HASMONEAN INDEPENDENCE AND RULE

While Israel's Hasmonean family ruled Israel, they may have encouraged the development of Hebrew Scripture by combining the Torah with historical, prophetic, and wisdom literature. In later centuries, Christians called the text the Old Testament.

63 BCE: JERUSALEM ENTERED BY ROMANS

The Romans took control of Israel and called the area Palestine.

4 BCE—30 CE: LIFETIME OF JESUS OF NAZARETH

70 CE: DESTRUCTION OF JERUSALEM'S SECOND TEMPLE BY THE ROMANS

135 CE: BANISHMENT OF JEWS FROM JERUSALEM BY THE ROMANS

Appendix B

Questions for Reflection and Discussion

PART I. LIVING IN GOD'S IMAGE

Chapter 1. Created in God's Image

1. What does it mean to you to be created in God's image?
2. How do the historical origins of the creation story affect your understanding of creation in God's image?
3. If you ever felt displaced and discouraged like the Babylonian exiles, what helped you regain your confidence?
4. How does the notion of creation in God's image affect the way you regard other people?

Chapter 2. Happiness in the Garden of Eden

1. How have you experienced a sacred, spiritual, or otherwise special dimension in your life?
2. How do you relate to the different ways God is portrayed in the garden of Eden, other parts of the Bible, and our culture today?
3. To what extent does Adam and Eve's life in the garden of Eden represent your vision of the bonds among people, the earth, and divinity?
4. When have you experienced moral, altruistic, supercharged relationships?

Chapter 3. Darkness outside the Garden

1. To what extent are Adam and Eve representative of the way you view human nature?
2. How does the ancient Near Eastern wisdom tradition, combined with the harshness of Israelite life, affect your view of Adam and Eve's story?
3. How does the dark side of human nature influence you to act contrary to your values?
4. What can you do to protect yourself and others from violence and abuse?

Chapter 4. Justice and Compassion in Noah's Flood

1. How does the flood story affect your view of God?
2. When would the scribes' view of mercy be helpful to you in your personal life or community?
3. When would the priests' view of justice be helpful to you in your personal life or community?
4. When have you found it particularly difficult to balance justice with mercy?

PART II. TAKING A JOURNEY

Chapter 5. Abraham Counting the Stars

1. How do you identify with the people in Abraham's story?
2. How does the influence of the Israelite exiles affect your view of Abraham's story?
3. Have you ever felt a sacred presence or other force beyond yourself guide you toward a better way of life?
4. How would you envision God or some spiritual presence breaking into your life?

QUESTIONS FOR REFLECTION AND DISCUSSION

Chapter 6. Calling for Isaac's Sacrifice

1. How does the historical context affect your view of Isaac's near sacrifice?
2. How do you relate to Abraham's courage to live by his deepest values?
3. How do you relate to Isaac's resilience despite a horrific ordeal?
4. How can you find enduring values in the Bible despite changing cultural norms?

Chapter 7. Jacob Wrestling with God

1. How do you relate to Jacob as a trickster?
2. How do you relate to Jacob as a patriarch favored by God?
3. When have you felt as though you were wrestling with God, your conscience, or other forces beyond yourself?
4. How do your strengths and weaknesses affect your personal aspirations and spiritual life?

Chapter 8. Divine Providence in Joseph's Life

1. How have you prevailed despite efforts to undermine you?
2. How do you respond to biblical passages about God staying behind the scenes instead of appearing and speaking to people in the passages?
3. To what extent do you agree with the wisdom tradition of the ancient Near East?
4. To what extent do you believe in an underlying force that brings about a positive outcome over time despite setbacks facing you, your community, or the world?

Appendix B

PART III. FINDING REDEMPTION

Chapter 9. Overcoming Adversity

1. How does the development of the exodus story from a historical perspective affect your view of the story and its significance to you?
2. How do you relate the exodus story to challenges that you have overcome in your life?
3. How do you relate the exodus story to your efforts to help others overcome adversity?
4. When you struggle for freedom, justice, and fairness, what discourages you, and what gives you hope?

Chapter 10. Celebrating a Peaceful Victory

1. In what circumstances do you find the concept of God as a divine warrior empowering, and in what circumstances do you find the concept destructive?
2. How have you encouraged fair and peaceful resolutions to conflicts in your relationships, and which approaches have been the most successful?
3. If you ever had to choose between reconciling, staying on guard, or leaving a destructive relationship, what did you choose and why?
4. How have your spiritual views helped or hindered you in finding constructive ways to deal with difficult people?

Chapter 11. Making It through the Wilderness

1. In what ways do you identify with the Israelites making the transition from slaves to God's people?
2. When you have overcome challenges, how has it affected your view of yourself, your way of life, and your faith?

QUESTIONS FOR REFLECTION AND DISCUSSION

3. What are the most powerful spiritual and community resources you have found to overcome adversity in your personal life?

4. How have your spiritual views, biblical teachings, or other ethical standards influenced your life story?

PART IV. PICTURING THE PROMISED LAND

Chapter 12. Drawing Close to God

1. How does Leviticus affect your view of Yom Kippur and Easter?

2. How do you draw close to God or whatever you consider most sacred?

3. How do you admit your shortcomings and make amends, and what makes you feel forgiven, accepted, and free?

4. How have you or your friends, family, or congregation developed rituals to express a spiritual dimension in your lives?

Chapter 13. Blessings for the Journey

1. How do you account for the appeal of the priestly blessing in Numbers from ancient to modern times?

2. To what extent are the concerns of the Israelites in the spy mission comparable to your concerns today about your life or faith?

3. How do you balance trust and mistrust, courage and fear, hope and despair in your life?

4. What calms you down in stressful circumstances?

Chapter 14. Centering Our Lives

1. How do you relate the Shema or Great Commandment to your life?

2. How does the historical context of the scribes writing Deuteronomy affect your views of its relevance for your life today?

3. How have spiritual values been passed along in your family from one generation to the next?
4. What insights does your generation bring to understanding a sacred quality of life?

Chapter 15. Choosing the Best Way

1. What does it mean to you to choose between "life and prosperity" or "death and adversity" in Deuteronomy?
2. How are your views of Deuteronomy affected by ancient Near Eastern concern for the disadvantaged and the Israelite exilic concept of human repentance and divine forgiveness?
3. What motivates you to live humbly with gratitude, generosity, and compassion?
4. What gives you a sense of purpose and fulfillment?

Appendix C

Organizing a Discussion Group

DISCUSSION GROUPS ARE A great way to broaden and deepen our spiritual perspectives. You might get together with a few friends to discuss this book, or you could suggest it to a book group with diverse religious and secular views. If you are a member of a church, you could discuss this book in an adult education class or small group, and you could invite religiously unaffiliated neighbors to join the discussion. You could also organize a discussion between two congregations of different faiths, inviting each congregation to suggest a book for discussion.

INITIAL CONSIDERATIONS

The discussions will be shaped by the religious and secular perspectives of the participants and the type of group you choose. By seeking people with diverse religious and secular views, you may find that the discussions will expand and enrich your spiritual views. If the discussions occur in an established church or book group, the group may follow its customary format or change it for these discussions. For example, if a church group usually begins and ends discussions with a prayer, it may want to modify this approach if people with different faiths and secular views are included. Other considerations include how many participants, when and where to meet, how often to meet, and whether refreshments will be served. One person is likely to lead the organizational efforts with assistance and feedback from other participants.

Appendix C

SETTING THE TONE

Everyone should feel their opinions are valued. The point of a discussion is to help people think through and express their views, listen to the views of others, and come to a deeper understanding of the issues. No one should make dismissive remarks to another person or try to convince other people to change their minds.

DISCUSSION QUESTIONS

The discussion group leader, with input from participants, should suggest questions that are most likely to appeal to the group. This book suggests questions at the beginning of each chapter and in the appendix. Depending on the group's schedule, the entire book could be discussed in one session, each part of the book could be discussed in four sessions, each chapter could be discussed in fifteen sessions, or the chapters could be grouped to fit the desired number of sessions. The discussion could begin with open-ended questions, such as "What did you find especially meaningful in the biblical story and how it was written?"

PERSONAL REFLECTIONS

This book is intended to help people relate the biblical stories to their personal lives. To help you connect the stories to your life, I discuss ways the stories enrich my life and the lives of my friends and family. If you talk about how the biblical stories relate to your own experiences, it may help you clarify your personal story and help others see connections with their lives. But no one should feel pressure to reveal their individual experiences, and if they do, their privacy should be respected outside of the group.

Appendix D

Biblical Passages by Scribes and Priests about the Flood

Below are passages about the flood in Genesis by the scribes and priests. The priests' version of the flood is reported in Genesis 6:9–22; 7:6, 11, 13–16a, 18–21, 24; 8:1–2a, 3–5, 14–19; 9:1–19, 28–29. The scribes' version is found in the rest of Genesis 6:5—9:29. The scribes refer to God by his name, Yahweh, which is conventionally translated as "Lord," with the initial large capital letter followed by small capital letters. By contrast, the priests use a more generic term, which is translated as "God." The attribution of passages to the scribes and priests is found in David M. Carr, "Genesis," in Coogan, *New Oxford Annotated Bible*, notes on 1:1—11:26 and 9:18–29.

SCRIBES' STORY ABOUT THE FLOOD IN GENESIS 6:5–8; 7:1–3, 12; 8:6–12, 20–22

Genesis 6:5

The Lord saw that the wickedness of humans was great in the earth and that every inclination of the thoughts of their hearts was only evil continually. ⁶And the Lord was sorry that he had made humans on the earth, and it grieved him to his heart. ⁷So the Lord said, "I will blot out from the earth the humans I have created—people together with animals and creeping things and birds of the air—for I am sorry that I have made them." ⁸But Noah found favor in the sight of the Lord.

Appendix D

Genesis 7:1

Then the Lord said to Noah, "Go into the ark, you and all your household, for I have seen that you alone are righteous before me in this generation. ²Take with you seven pairs of all clean animals, the male and its mate; and a pair of the animals that are not clean, the male and its mate; ³and seven pairs of the birds of the air also, male and female, to keep their kind alive on the face of all the earth.
¹²The rain fell on the earth forty days and forty nights.

Genesis 8:6

At the end of forty days Noah opened the window of the ark that he had made ⁷and sent out the raven, and it went to and fro until the waters were dried up from the earth. ⁸Then he sent out the dove from him to see if the waters had subsided from the face of the ground, ⁹but the dove found no place to set its foot, and it returned to him to the ark, for the waters were still on the face of the whole earth. So he put out his hand and took it and brought it into the ark with him. ¹⁰He waited another seven days, and again he sent out the dove from the ark, ¹¹and the dove came back to him in the evening, and there in its beak was a freshly plucked olive leaf; so Noah knew that the waters had subsided from the earth. ¹²Then he waited another seven days, and sent out the dove, and it did not return to him any more.
²⁰Then Noah built an altar to the Lord and took of every clean animal and of every clean bird and offered burnt offerings on the altar. ²¹And when the Lord smelled the pleasing odor, the Lord said in his heart, "I will never again curse the ground because of humans, for the inclination of the human heart is evil from youth; nor will I ever again destroy every living creature as I have done.
²²As long as the earth endures, / seedtime and harvest, cold and heat, / summer and winter, day and night, / shall not cease."

PRIESTS' STORY ABOUT THE FLOOD IN GENESIS 6:9B, 11, 13A, 18B–19, 22; 7:11B, 18, 24; 8:1–2A; 9:1, 6, 8–13, 18A–19, 29

Genesis 6:9b

Noah was a righteous man, blameless in his generation; Noah walked with God.
¹¹Now the earth was corrupt in God's sight, and the earth was filled with violence. ¹³ᵃAnd God said to Noah, . . . ¹⁸ᵇ "[You] shall come into the ark, you, your sons, your wife, and your sons' wives with you. ¹⁹And of every living thing, of all flesh, you shall bring two of every kind into the ark, to keep them alive with you; they shall be male and female. . . ." ²²Noah did this; he did all that God commanded him.

Genesis 7:11b

on that day all the fountains of the great deep burst forth, and the windows of the heavens were opened.
¹⁸The waters swelled and increased greatly on the earth, and the ark floated on the face of the waters. ²⁴And the waters swelled on the earth for one hundred fifty days.

Genesis 8:1

But God remembered Noah and all the wild animals and all the domestic animals that were with him in the ark. And God made a wind blow over the earth, and the waters subsided; ²ᵃthe fountains of the deep and the windows of the heavens were closed, . . .

Genesis 9:1

God blessed Noah and his sons and said to them, "Be fruitful and multiply, and fill the earth. ⁶Whoever sheds the blood of a human, / by a human shall that person's blood be shed; / for in his own image /God made humans. . . ." ⁸Then God said to Noah and to his sons with him, ⁹"As for me, I am establishing my covenant with you and your descendants after you ¹⁰and with every living creature that is with you, the birds, the domestic

Appendix D

animals, and every animal of the earth with you, as many as came out of the ark. ¹¹I establish my covenant with you, that never again shall all flesh be cut off by the waters of a flood, and never again shall there be a flood to destroy the earth." ¹²God said, "This is the sign of the covenant that I make between me and you and every living creature that is with you, for all future generations: ¹³I have set my bow in the clouds, and it shall be a sign of the covenant between me and the earth. . . ."

¹⁸ᵃ'The sons of Noah who went out of the ark were Shem, Ham, and Japheth. . . . ¹⁹'These three were the sons of Noah, and from these the whole earth was peopled.

²⁹All the days of Noah were nine hundred fifty years, and he died.

Bibliography

Amar, Akhil Reed. "The End of Roe v. Wade." *Wall Street Journal*, May 14, 2022. https://www.wsj.com/articles/the-end-of-roe-v-wade-11652453609.
Attridge, Harold W., ed. *The HarperCollins Study Bible including Apocryphal Deuterocanonical Books*. Rev. ed. New York: HarperCollins, 2006.
Benedict XVI, Pope. "General Audience." Vatican, May 25, 2011. https://www.vatican.va/content/benedict-xvi/en/audiences/2011/documents/hf_ben-xvi_aud_20110525.html/.
———. *Verbum Domini: The Word of God in the Life and Mission of the Church*. Frederick, MD: Word among Us, 2010.
Berlin, Adele, and Marc Zvi Brettler, eds. *The Jewish Study Bible*. 2nd ed. Jewish Publication Society Tanakh Translation. New York: Oxford University Press, 2014.
Black, C. Clifton. *The Lord's Prayer*. Interpretation. Louisville: Westminster John Knox, 2018.
The Book of Confessions. Part 1 of *The Constitution of the Presybterian Church (U.S.A.)*. Louisville: Office of the General Assembly, 2016. https://www.pcusa.org/site_media/media/uploads/oga/pdf/boc2016.pdf.
Brueggemann, Walter. *Genesis*. Interpretation. Atlanta: John Knox, 1982.
Carr, David M. *The Hebrew Bible: A Contemporary Introduction to the Christian Old Testament and the Jewish Tanakh*. 2nd ed. Hoboken, NJ: Wiley-Blackwell, 2021.
———. *Holy Resilience: The Bible's Traumatic Origins*. New Haven: Yale University Press, 2014.
———. *An Introduction to the Old Testament: Sacred Texts and Imperial Contexts of the Hebrew Bible*. Malden, MA: Wiley-Blackwell, 2010.
———. *Writing on the Tablet of the Heart: Origins of Scripture and Literature*. New York: Oxford University Press, 2005.
Childs, Brevard S. *The Book of Exodus: A Critical, Theological Commentary*. Old Testament Library. Philadelphia: Westminster, 1974.
Coogan, Michael D., ed. *The New Oxford Annotated Bible: New Revised Standard Version with the Apocrypha*. 5th ed. New York: Oxford University Press, 2018.
Cooper, Alan. "A Medieval Jewish Version of Original Sin: Ephraim of Luntshits on Leviticus 12." *Harvard Theological Review* 97 (2004) 445–59. https://www.researchgate.net/

BIBLIOGRAPHY

publication/231840434_A_Medieval_Jewish_Version_of_Original_Sin_Ephraim_of_Luntshits_on_Leviticus_12/.

Dawood, N. J., trans. *The Koran.* London: Penguin, 2006.

Dorfner, Micah. "Mayo Mindfulness: Grow Happiness through Focus and Practice." Mayo Clinic News Network, May 23, 2018. https://newsnetwork.mayoclinic.org/discussion/mayo-mindfulness-grow-happiness-through-focus-and-practice/.

Erikson, Erik H. *Childhood and Society.* 2nd ed. New York: Norton, 1963.

———. *Insight and Responsibility: Lectures on the Ethical Implications of Psychoanalytic Insight.* New York: Norton, 1964.

Feld, Edward, et al. *Mahzor Lev Shalem for Rosh Hashanah and Yom Kippur.* New York: Rabbinical Assembly, 2010.

Fitzgerald, Allan D., ed. *Augustine through the Ages: An Encyclopedia.* Grand Rapids: Eerdmans, 1999.

Gaustad, Edwin, and Leigh Schmidt. *The Religious History of America: The Heart of the American Story from Colonial Times to Today.* Rev. ed. New York: HarperOne, 2002.

Gowan, Donald E. *From Eden to Babel: A Commentary on the Book of Genesis 1–11.* Grand Rapids: Eerdmans, 1988.

Greenspahn, Frederick E., ed. *Essential Papers on Israel and the Ancient Near East.* New York: New York University Press, 1991.

Hayes, Christine. *Introduction to the Bible.* New Haven: Yale University Press, 2012.

Herman, Judith. *Trauma and Recovery: The Aftermath of Violence—From Domestic Abuse to Political Terror.* New York: Basic, 2015.

Jacobs, Louis. *The Book of Jewish Belief.* New York: Behrman, 1984.

The Jewish Theological Seminary of America et al. *Emet ve-Emunah: Statement of Principles of Conservative Judaism.* N.p.: N.p., 1988. https://www.bjpa.org/search-results/publication/18660.

King, L. W., trans. "The Code of Hammurabi." Avalon Project, 2008. avalon.law.yale.edu/ancient/hamframe.asp.

Kugel, James L. *The Great Shift: Encountering God in Biblical Times.* Boston: Houghton Mifflin Harcourt, 2017.

———. *How to Read the Bible: A Guide to Scripture, Then and Now.* New York: Free, 2007.

Lawson, Christine Ann. *Understanding the Borderline Mother: Helping Her Children Transcend the Intense, Unpredictable, and Volatile Relationship.* Lanham, MD: Rowman & Littlefield, 2004.

Levenson, Jon D. *The Death and Resurrection of the Beloved Son: The Transformation of Child Sacrifice in Judaism and Christianity.* New Haven: Yale University Press, 1993.

Marchese, David. "Yale's Happiness Professor Says Anxiety Is Destroying Her Students." *New York Times Magazine,* Feb. 18, 2022. https://www.nytimes.com/interactive/2022/02/21/magazine/laurie-santos-interview.html.

Matthews, Victor H., and Don C. Benjamin. *Old Testament Parallels: Laws and Stories from the Ancient Near East.* 4th ed. New York: Paulist, 2016.

McAdams, Dan P. *The Redemptive Self: Stories Americans Live By.* Rev. and exp. ed. New York: Oxford University Press, 2013.

Migliore, Daniel L. *Faith Seeking Understanding: An Introduction to Christian Theology.* 3rd ed. Grand Rapids: Eerdmans, 2014.

National Scientific Council on the Developing Child. *Supportive Relationships and Active Skill-Building Strengthen the Foundations of Resilience.* Working Paper 13. Center on

Bibliography

the Developing Child, May 2015. https://developingchild.harvard.edu/wp-content/uploads/2015/05/The-Science-of-Resilience.pdf.

Norton, Mary Beth, et al. *To 1877.* Vol. 1 of *A People and a Nation: A History of the United States.* 8th ed. Boston: Houghton Mifflin, 2008.

Pinker, Steven. *The Better Angels of Our Nature: Why Violence Has Declined.* New York: Penguin, 2011.

Putnam, Robert D., and David E. Campbell. *American Grace: How Religion Divides and Unites Us.* New York: Simon & Schuster, 2010.

Rotelle, John E., OSA, ed. *Sermons 148–83.* Translated by Edmund Hill OP. Vol. 5 of *Part 3—Sermons.* The Works of Saint Augustine: A Translation for the 21st Century. New Rochelle, NY: New City Press, 1992. https://wesleyscholar.com/wp-content/uploads/2019/04/Augustine-Sermons-148-183.pdf.

Sanadiki, Khaled. *Legends & Narratives of Islam: The Biblical Personalities.* Chicago: Kazi, 2000.

Smith, Christian, and Amy Adamczyk. *Handing Down the Faith: How Parents Pass Their Religion on to the Next Generation.* New York: Oxford University Press, 2021.

Smith, Huston. *The World's Religions: Our Great Wisdom Traditions.* 2nd ed. New York: HarperOne, 1991.

Sparks, Dana. "Mayo Mindfulness: Connecting Spirituality and Stress Relief." Mayo Clinic News Network, Apr. 3, 2019. https://newsnetwork.mayoclinic.org/discussion/mayo-mindfulness-connecting-spirituality-and-stress-relief.

Trible, Phyllis. *God and the Rhetoric of Sexuality.* Overtures to Biblical Theology. Philadelphia: Fortress, 1978.

———. *Texts of Terror: Literary-Feminist Readings of Biblical Narratives.* Overtures to Biblical Theology. Philadelphia: Fortress, 1984.

Westermann, Claus. *Genesis.* Translated by David E. Green. London: T. & T. Clark, 2004.

White, Matthew. *The Great Big Book of Horrible Things: The Definitive Chronicle of History's 100 Worst Atrocities.* New York: Norton, 2012.

Wiesel, Elie. *Messengers of God: Biblical Portraits and Legends.* Translated by Marion Wiesel. New York: Simon & Schuster, 1976.

Williams, Delores S. *Sisters in the Wilderness: The Challenge of Womanist God-Talk.* Maryknoll, NY: Orbis, 1993.

www.ingramcontent.com/pod-product-compliance
Lightning Source LLC
Chambersburg PA
CBHW030856170426
43193CB00009BA/635